MW00712658

Lazarus still Rises

True Stories of Faith and Miracles Happening in the
Lives of God's People Today

Barbara J. Cornelius

Lazarus Still Rises

Copyright © 2010 Barbara J. Cornelius

All rights reserved/No part of this book may be reproduced or utilized in any form or by any means, electronic or mechanical, including photocopying and recording, or by any information storage and retrieval system, without permission in writing from the author.

ISBN: 978-0-9818252-5-0
Library of Congress PCN: 2010933537

Cover art and interior illustrations by Jane McNeil
Cover and interior design and formatting by Dekie Hicks

Wheredepony Press
Rome, GA 30162
www.wheredeponypress.com

Manufactured in the United States of America

All scripture quotations unless otherwise indicated, are taken from *The Holy Bible, New Living Translation*, copyright © 1966. Used by the permission of Tyndale House Publishers, Inc. Wheaton, Illinois 60189. All rights reserved.

Scripture taken from the *New King James Version*. Copyright ©1982 by Thomas Nelson, Inc. Used by permission. All rights reserved.

Scripture taken from *THE MESSAGE*. Copyright © 2003 by Eugene H. Pererson. Used by permission of NavPress Publishing Group.

Scripture taken from *The Holy Bible, English Standard Version*, copyright ©2001 by Crossway Bibles, a division of Good News Publishers. Used by permission. All rights reserved.

wheredepony

ACKNOWLEDGEMENTS

I am very grateful to my husband, Larry Cornelius, for his insights and contribution to this book. Larry has brightened my life for over forty years and his love and support have given me the encouragement I needed to record these life-changing revelations of my heart.

I would like to also thank my mother, Martha Spencer, for her love and courage which helped shape my life. My daughter, Jennifer, son-in-law Earl, son Jeff, and daughter-in-law Julie are truly gifts from the living God. The Lord has drenched me in blessings with my sister Sue Hannah and brother-in-law Morris Hannah and the birth of my seven grandchildren: Brandon Wyatt, Alyssa Wyatt, Jacie Snipes, Benjamin Snipes, Abigail Cornelius, Jeffrey Cornelius, and Robert Cornelius. May they carry God's light inside them every day of their lives and be blessings to His kingdom.

My father Harold Spencer and colleague Mike Lee inspired me to be a teacher who taught from the heart. May every reader who is a teacher and every person who aspires to work with children be blessed by their stories.

I would also like to thank my pastor, Dr. Shelia Bookout, for her witness of what the Lord has done in her life through her trials and tribulations. Her walk in courage has inspired me to also walk in faith through the valleys of my own life.

Most of all, I want to thank the Lord Jesus for what He has meant to my life. I have felt His presence since the age of twelve, and despite all of my human failings, He has taught me to walk in victory through His power and light in me. Praise God!

TABLE OF CONTENTS

Lazarus Still Rises

Introduction

*B*oth the Old and New Testaments describe many miracles that happened as the living God interceded on behalf of His people. Are miracles still happening today? Is God still acting on our behalf?

I know He is still giving the gift of miracles because I have witnessed them all my life. I have wept when God seemed to be silent and non-responsive to my prayers for friends, loved ones, and even strangers. In those circumstances, I have come to realize that the miracles I prayed for happened in ways that I could neither see nor comprehend. Yet, when God intercedes in human events and defies logic, laws of physics, and man's expectations, He thrills our souls!

Not long ago, the whole world watched as a plane crash-landed in the Hudson River, missing a bridge by only 900 feet. It was the first crash-landing on water in over forty years which was accomplished safely, and in one of God's "coincidences," the plane's pilot was also a skilled glider pilot. An error of only one degree in his maneuvering would have brought disaster. All 155 people on board were rescued and the world marveled as the details were revealed. As the plane filled with water, boats quickly arrived and all the passengers were rescued.

Surely as that plane was filled with the passengers' prayers, God sent His angels to safely land the plane in the water. I wonder if He does things like that to ask the world if it is paying attention and if people have any realization of who He is. Do people today have any awareness of the omnipotent, holy, and all powerful living God?

I have been aware of God's angels all my life. I have not personally seen them, but I have seen their work in delivering God's people from peril. I once prayed with a group of believers in a Bible study to have God show us His glory. That week I saw the form of two archangels in the clouds, and another person in the study found a white feather at her mail box. Everyone in this group believed that our prayer was answered.

We surely see God's miracles in the way He brings deliverance and redemption from sin in our lives, and on some occasions, He does something spectacular and surprising that floods our hearts with joy. His miracles are occurring all the time. They are happening through people He puts in our lives to bless us, through situations the world calls coincidences, and through the healing of our crushed spirits. The God of today is the same God written about in the Bible. The blessing of spiritual vision enables us to see the hand of God acting on our behalf everyday!

God's light has been passed through many generations in my family. It is my heart's desire to leave this book as a memorial stone to His presence in the lives of family members, friends, and others who have been a part of my life's experiences.

May every person who reads this book receive spiritual blessings and may God's kingdom be called forth in their lives!

BARBARA J. CORNELIUS

John 11:41-44

So they rolled the stone aside. Then Jesus looked up to heaven and said, "Father, thank you for hearing me. You always hear me, but I said it out loud for the sake of all these people standing here, so they will believe you sent me." Then Jesus shouted, "Lazarus, come out!" And Lazarus came out, bound in graveclothes, his face wrapped in a headcloth. Jesus told them, "Unwrap him and let him go!"

Psalm 118:17

I will not die, but I will live to tell what the LORD has done.

James 5:14-15

Are any among you sick? They should call for the elders of the church and have them pray over them, anointing them with oil in the name of the Lord. And their prayer offered in faith will heal the sick, and the Lord will make them well...

CHAPTER ONE

Jamie's Story

Miracle of a Young Man Saved from Death

A twenty-three year old man lay in a hospital bed in intensive care surrounded by family members. He was found unconscious by his roommate who thought at first that he was just sleeping late. He didn't realize that an accidental combination of drugs caused his friend to be at death's door

Jamie was in a coma and one of his doctors sadly told his parents, "Jamie most likely will not survive. If he doesn't die, I fear he will be severely brain-damaged because of probable extreme oxygen deprivation." Hope was not part of the doctor's words.

What his doctors could not know was that Jamie's family was blessed with a personal relationship with Jesus Christ, and their expectations were not based on medical science. Just as Jesus had been summoned to the bedside of his friend Lazarus all those hundreds of years ago, Jamie's family summoned Jesus to be at Jamie's bedside. When Jesus arrived for Lazarus, he had been dead four days. Faith would defy logic.

When Jamie's parents called upon Jesus, they were defying logic and raising their shields of faith. With these shields they fought to quench every "fiery dart" that Satan was sending toward their loved one.

Jamie's parents were not alone. Many people, who also loved Jamie but were not at his side, bombarded heaven with their prayers, pleading for Jesus to heal him. Young people who loved Jamie came to the hospital and stayed for hours in the intensive care waiting room.

One young woman summoned her friends to escort her to the chapel in the hospital and pray aloud to Jesus. "Make some noise to my Jesus!" she said. She didn't know if her friends knew Jesus, but she was determined that they would find out about Him through Jamie's healing.

Jamie's stepbrother, Adam, stayed at his bedside, refusing to leave him. The Lord had given Adam a deep love for the young man whom he considered his brother. Jamie was not a brother of his blood, but more importantly, he was the brother of his heart. Adam was not going to leave him because he believed that somehow his presence at Jamie's bedside would prevent him from slipping into eternity.

After several days of being in a coma, Jamie's kidneys and liver began to fail. The medical staff tried to wean him off the ventilator, but they were not successful. After a week of nothing but failure to restore Jamie to full consciousness, hope seemed to be an unreasonable gift to possess.

Jamie's stepmother, Gloria, and I have been friends for thirty-five years, and we claim each other as sisters. I went to the hospital to offer my support, and to pray with the family in the waiting area. While I was with them, I gave them a symbol of encouragement.

It was a "Clinging Cross"[1] that fits perfectly in the palm of one's hand.

This cross has given comfort to thousands of people and the credit for the design of this cross was given by Jane Davis in 2003 to God Himself. I told Jamie's parents, "Hold this cross while you pray for Jamie and give it to him when he awakens."

6

Jamie's parents then invited me to pray for him in his intensive care room.

Upon entering the room, I did something I had not done before. Sometimes boldness in faith comes with a situation so desperate that your inhibitions melt away. I anointed the unconscious Jamie with oil and began praying at his bedside. I petitioned the Lord to heal Jamie and surround him with angels. As I prayed for him, I saw something amazing! Tears were streaming down his cheeks and it seemed that at some level in his spirit, he was responding to the spoken words.

While Jamie was hospitalized, some of the angels that were present were nurses who prayed over him and gave prophecy of his healing. One nurse disagreed with the doctors' dire predictions and told his family, "It looks like you will be getting your boy back!" Jamie was never ever alone, for the mighty living God Himself was there at his bedside. He summoned His people filled with His Holy Spirit to prayer, and He also sent His angels, unseen but mighty in their presence, to stand guard at Jamie's side.

A couple of days after my time with Jamie, Joseph, a friend of our family and a great prayer warrior, met my son and me at the hospital. Joseph and his wife, Karen, had come to the United States five years previously from Ghana, Africa. I had prayed for the Lord to send a male Christian advocate for my son, and the Lord sent this wonderful man of great faith. Joseph and Karen have sacrificed greatly to remain in this country, and the hand of the living God placed Joseph at Jamie's bedside.

The day Joseph came to the hospital, I met him in the reception area and told him, "There is fear that before Jamie arrived at the hospital, he suffered severe brain damage." Joseph looked at me intently and selected scripture from his Bible. The three of us then went to the intensive care waiting room and met Jamie's parents. With great conviction resonating in his voice, Joseph read aloud the story of Lazarus from John 11:1-45, and all of us claimed this scripture for Jamie's healing.

When Joseph entered Jamie's room, he anointed him with

oil and prayed for God to heal him and remove any infirmity in his body, after which he claimed Psalm 118:17 for Jamie's witness: "I will not die, but I will live to tell what the Lord has done." He then walked over to the white message board on the wall and recorded this scripture as a message of faith for all to see.

A few days later, after several failed attempts to remove Jamie from the ventilator, another try was successful and a miracle occurred! Jamie awoke and began talking to his family. His mother gave him his "Clinging Cross", and surprisingly Jamie recognized it as his. Later the cross fell to the floor and broke into two pieces, but his father glued it back together and handed it to him. The symbolism for the cross was complete. Jamie was broken, but the sacrifice of Jesus on the cross had made him whole again.

After being either unconscious or semiconscious for twelve days, Jamie stunned everyone that first day of being awake by ordering a full lunch and devouring it. Doctors continued to be shocked when his liver and kidney functions became perfectly normal in a few days.

I went to the hospital a couple of days later to pray a prayer of praise with Jamie and his parents. I know the living God smiles when we remember to thank Him for giving us our heart's desires. He is omnipotent and all powerful, but we can still delight him with our prayers of thanksgiving and praise. I gave Jamie slips of paper with his scripture on them: Psalm 118:17. Later, with a grateful heart, Jamie handed one to each person who entered his hospital room symbolizing how the Lord would use him to spread His word for His kingdom's glory.

Jamie's story is still being written as God calls to him, as his parents and friends continue to pray for him, and as he seeks God's will for his life. God finds Jamie, in his weaknesses, perfect for His kingdom's work, for it is through his weaknesses that the power of the living God is seen vividly.

Rest assured that Satan will try very hard to diminish the memory and impact of Jamie's miraculous healing. Prayers will cover Jamie all the days of his life, prayers that Satan will not be given any ground and that Jamie's steps will be directed, so his footprints will bring others to the healing offered by our Savior, Jesus Christ

There are a multitude of stories like Jamie's which demonstrate that the living God is still doing miracles today, miracles like those we have read about in the Bible. I have witnessed miracles all my life, and I fervently desire to glorify the Lord by writing more about what He has done.

Psalm 91:1, 11-12 *

He who dwells in the secret place of the Most High Shall abide under the shadow of the Almighty.

For He shall give His angels charge over you, To keep you in all your ways. In their hands they shall bear you up, Lest you dash your foot against a stone.

* New King James Version

CHAPTER TWO

Defying the Laws of Physics

Miracle on a Four-Lane Highway

*S*eeing Jamie defy his doctors' predictions for his physical demise is just one of many miracles I have witnessed in my lifetime. One of the most dramatic miracles I experienced was over forty years ago when I was twenty-two years old.

I was driving on a four-lane highway near my home when I saw a wheel from my car fly off ahead of me! For a moment I had a vision of the 500 mile race held in Indianapolis, Indiana, every year. There was just one small problem with the vision; I was not a race car driver. I was a first-year teacher returning home from school.

A short time previously, I had noticed there seemed to be some unusual sound coming from the car as I sped down the road that day. I even stopped at a service station and inquired about what I was hearing. I was told I would have to wait for quite awhile because they were busy, and they would need to put the car on a rack to examine it. Furthermore, with only the vague information I was able to provide them, it might take considerable time to determine the cause of the noise. Realizing I was only a few minutes from home, I allowed my impatience to overrule prudence as I decided not to wait.

A few minutes later as I was traveling down the highway at fifty miles per hour, a rear wheel flew off the car and past my windshield. When I lost the wheel, I also lost control of my car, and I frantically turned the steering wheel in my attempt to stay on the road. There was traffic all around me that day, and even though I somehow managed to miss all of it, I soon found myself heading over a very steep embankment, and I knew I was going to die. I was only married a few months, and I realized I was about to leave my young husband a widower. As I processed those thoughts, I experienced no fear and even felt a sense of calm in my spirit.

Suddenly the car, without any sign of slowing down, turned around and stopped at a right angle across the highway. It was as if a very strong giant had grabbed the bumper before the car reached the edge of the embankment! I climbed out of the car and stood on the side of the road with my knees knocking together. When I glanced at my wrists, I saw scratches from my fingernails where I had been frantically turning the steering wheel.

In a few minutes a police car with two officers came by. One of the officers looked at my stricken face and said, "Come and sit in our vehicle, and we will see what we can do to help you." As I sat trembling in their car, they searched for the wheel and the lug nuts that had separated themselves from my vehicle. I couldn't believe they could possibly find them on the long stretch of the highway and the grassy area next to it. Surprisingly, they found three of the four lug nuts and the wheel which they put back on my car.

While I was waiting, a truck driver stopped by and told the police officers, "That young lady did an amazing job of keeping her car on the road!" I will always be grateful to that truck driver, for not only did he stop and take time to share his encouraging observations with the officers, he also gave me a witness to ponder all my life. Surely I had supernatural assistance that day to survive impending death.

I had very little driving experience at the time of my accident, and that caused me to be a very timid driver. My father was very protective of me when I lived at home and would not allow me to drive in the rain or any distances longer than a few miles. One time when I was a teenager, I was driving on a gravel road at night, going a little too fast, and I ended up in the ditch. It took a nearby farmer with a tractor to pull me out. When I reached my early twenties, I never had a great desire to be the driver to any chosen location and was always grateful when someone else volunteered to drive. On the fateful day I lost my wheel, I knew I could not possibly have kept a three-wheeled car on the road by my own efforts.

The police officers shocked me when they put me back in my car and said, "Have a safe trip home." I expected them to realize I needed someone else to take me home. I was too numb to resist their instructions. Later I realized that if I had not driven home that day, it probably would have been quite some time before I would have possessed the courage to drive again. In those days there were no cell phones, so I couldn't call my husband and have him come retrieve me and drive me home. Those police officers did all the right things, but how could they have possibly known what they needed to do for me?

For an entire week after the accident, I felt I should have been dead. I didn't see how in the world I could have survived that ordeal. There was no good explanation for other vehicles not hitting me or for my car suddenly stopping and turning around. I was an elementary school teacher who loved teaching science, and I knew what had happened to me defied the laws of physics as I understood them.

A few years later, when I read Billy Graham's book, *Angels: God's Secret Agents* [2], I began to see that there was an explanation for my survival that would not be found in any science book. I began to believe the miraculous steering that kept the car on the road had to be done by an angel sitting next to me, and another angel must have reached out and grabbed the car by the bumper to keep it from going down the steep embankment.

I remember arriving home that day in my very agitated state and telling my husband about my near fatal accident. He looked at me with a very pained expression and said in a very quiet voice, "I changed that tire a few days ago and I must not have gotten the lug nuts entirely tightened." I can only imagine how much grief he would have experienced in his lifetime if the hand of God had not been on both of us that day. God was protecting him as much as he was protecting me!

I have lost a few friends over the years to automobile accidents, and I cannot explain why I was chosen to have divine assistance that day. I believe that the Lord had a plan for my life that did not include my death at that particular time. I also know that many things occur in our lives that will only be understood when our time on Earth is finished and we are home with the Lord.

Sometimes when someone dies in an accident and I wonder why he or she was not saved, the Lord says to me in my spirit, "You have no idea how many times My angels were called into action to protect this person on other occasions." I just know God revealed to me that day that He is in control. We cannot possibly explain the mind of God with our limited human intelligence and spiritual vision, and this is why we must trust Him with our lives.

David says of angels, "He who dwelleth in the secret place of the Most High shall abide under the shadow of the Almighty… For he shall give his angels charge over thee, to keep thee in all thy ways. They shall bear thee up…lest thou dash thy foot against a stone" (Psalm 91:1, 11-12). I know on that fateful day, there were angels watching over me.

All my life the Lord has amazed me with His defiance of logic and human reasoning. I know that if we give Him our hearts, our souls, our minds, and our strength, there is nothing we request in His name and for His kingdom's sake that He will deny.

In my daily prayers, in the authority and power of Jesus Christ, I summon God's angels to war for me and my entire family. I ask that they guard us at all times during the day, and in the name of Jesus, I release them to war for me and my household and provide protection against the evil one, that we might all participate in His kingdom's work. I know if circumstances prevail against my desire for health and safety for a loved one, and he leaves this earth in an untimely way, God's angels will be there with him.

Why Am I Here?

Father, tell me why am I here.
Why is there so much sickness
And why so much fear?
Please, why am I here?

Father, why is there so much sadness
And why so many a tear?
Please tell me why I am here.

Father, will I faithfully follow Thee
And fully for Thy cause will I plea,
Or will I be just another lost, not really ever free?

Father, let me tell others why we are here.
Let me share how You have given a way to forget all of
  our tears
And no longer hold on to our fears,
And through Your Son, find the reason for being here.

Written by Barbara J. Spencer (Cornelius)
Age 12

BARBARA J. CORNELIUS

1 Peter 1:4

For God has reserved a priceless inheritance for his children. It is kept in heaven for you, pure and undefiled, beyond the reach of change and decay.

Ephesians 2:7

And so God can always point to us as examples of the incredible wealth of his favor and kindness toward us, as shown in all he has done for us through Christ Jesus.

Philippians 4:19

And this same God who takes care of me will supply all your needs from his glorious riches, which have been given to us in Christ Jesus.

CHAPTER THREE

Millionaire Teacher

How to be a Millionaire without Money

"All right God, I am twelve years old and I don't know which career in life You have planned for me!" I have had lots of conversations with the Lord over the years, but I remember that one as if it happened yesterday. I always liked to plan my future far in advance, and I wanted to know as soon as possible in which direction I should look for my life's work. We did not have GPS navigation systems in those days, but if I could have secured a "spiritual GPS," I most certainly would have! I knew without any doubts one career that I did not want to select was that of a teacher. There had been many teachers in my family, and I thought teaching was a boring occupation.

When I was sixteen years old and a junior in high school, I still did not know what I was going to do when I graduated. Then

I became a pupil in Mr. Spencer's classroom. He was my social studies teacher, and he didn't seem to have much affection for the textbook issued for his class. His lesson plans were not found in a teacher's edition, but instead came from his inspiration about his subject matter. I still remember him saying, "Our forefathers' hands shook as they signed the Declaration of Independence because they realized the risks they were taking." He spoke with great emotion as he continued, "They risked their fortunes, their reputations and their very lives." Mr. Spencer had the remarkable ability to present to us the 200 year history of our country and make us feel like we were experiencing it right then in his class-room. It was as if he could go back in time to see and experience the events himself, and he wanted to bring us along for the trip.

For twenty-eight years, Mr. Spencer also announced and kept score at all the basketball games. He would say, "Good evening, basketball fans!" The crowd would roar back, "Good evening, Mr. Spencer!" One year when the team was having a winning streak, he made sure he wore the same pair of socks to every game. (I am not positive, but I believe they were washed between games!)

One winter during the Christmas break, he drove 500 miles over icy roads to return home from a trip in time for a tourna-ment game. He just knew the team needed him to be there in order for them to win, and he even visited the locker room at halftime with our team sixteen points behind. As he delivered an inspiring speech, he said, "I have traveled many treacher-ous miles to witness not your defeat but your stunning victory!" Amazingly, we won the game that night. When he retired, the field house was named the Spencer Field House. The name of the high school was Van Buren, and Mr. Spencer was such an integral part of the school that he was often referred to as "Mr. Van Buren." It was fitting for "Mr. Van Buren" to have his own field house.

He often talked about his family with his students. Six years before I became one of his students, he told a classroom, "I cannot stay and teach your class today because I must go home and watch my son die." He cried as he spoke with unusual bluntness. His only son was nine years old and had been ill for three years. This was the child to whom he had written messages while he was away in the Navy during World War ll. Even though his son was only three years old at the time, he asked him to look after his mother while Daddy was away. Now it was his son who was leaving him.

He once said that losing his son made him more compassionate as a teacher. He was known to recruit an entire classroom of students to support one student who was struggling to stay in school and complete requirements to graduate. He hadn't been able to save his son, but he could try and rescue students who came into his classroom from failing in the world. If there was a way to do that, he would find it. He enlisted any help he could

Despite the mountain of medical bills he had from his son's illness, he often purchased lunch for students who he knew could not afford it. There were no free lunches provided by the federal government in those days. Mr. Spencer had a heart for any student who had a need of any kind. Some felt that his helping so many others was a way to soften the pain of losing his precious son.

Mr. Spencer also volunteered to coach his students in softball because he so loved the sport. One year when he discovered that there was no money in the budget to buy equipment, he bought the required supplies himself. His students always had what they needed for every softball game, and they never knew the sacrifice he made to provide for them.

He owned only two suits during a time when teachers were required to wear suits to school daily, and he owned only one pair of shoes that had holes in the soles, but he was a very wealthy man in his spirit. He often said with a big smile on his face, "When I retire I am going to write a book entitled *How to be a Millionaire without a Million Dollars.*" He never got around to writing that book, but he lived the life of a rich man without much money. He knew what real wealth was, and it was reflected in the hundreds of young people in whom he invested his life.

Sometimes we are thrilled when we listen to a great musician play a beautiful, inspiring piece of music on the piano, watch a sports hero perform a great feat in the last moments of the game to bring his team to victory, or hear a speaker give a wonderfully inspirational speech. In those moments we wish that we too could perform extraordinary feats like those. Watching Mr. Spencer teach his classes and work with students was like having those kinds of experiences.

There was magic in his classroom and being there caused me to change my mind about teaching. I became filled with the desire to become a teacher and to create that kind of atmosphere for students in a classroom of my own. I wanted to emulate Mr. Spencer when he "kicked educational sixty-yard field goals" in his classrooms with his students.

Mr. Spencer infected me with a desire to touch young people in the inspiring way he did, and once I made the decision to become a teacher, I felt that had been the Lord's plan for my life all along. That decision lead to a long teaching career similar to Mr. Spencer's. He retired after thirty-eight years in the classroom. Sadly, he had health problems for many years and lived only two and half years after he retired.

He frequently told his students, "I do not want to 'rust out.' I want to 'wear out'. When the time comes for me to leave this earth, I want just one red rose on my casket." A former student who remembered hearing those words placed a single red rose inside his casket when he died. The town where he lived had a population of 10,000 people and over 1,000 came to the funeral home to say good-bye. After the funeral, the hearse carrying his body to the cemetery passed by the high school where he had spent so many years as a teacher. On the marquee next to the school, a simple message was posted, "Thank you, Mr. Spencer."

He died a very rich man because he could identify real treasure. I know all of this because Mr. Spencer was my father, and he left me a very large legacy-- a love for teaching and investing in the future of many generations of young people. His inspiration stayed with me during my entire thirty-seven year career in the classroom, and I loved what I did until the day I retired.

The Lord has given his people a priceless inheritance. May all of us who know the Lord die as very rich people because we know where real wealth is to be found! Let us leave a precious legacy with our testimony to the incredible wealth of God's favor.

Romans 8:10

Since Christ lives within you, even though your body will die because of sin, your spirit is alive because you have been made right with God.

1 Corinthians 2:12

And God has actually given us his Spirit (not the world's spirit) so we can know the wonderful things God has freely given us.

2 Chronicles 7:1

When Solomon finished praying, fire flashed down from heaven and burned up the burnt offerings and sacrifices, and the glorious presence of the LORD filled the Temple.

CHAPTER FOUR

Annointed Classroom

God in My Classroom

*K*nowing I was called to be a teacher like my father gave me the belief that the Lord would always have a plan for my teaching assignments. I knew I could trust Him with placing me where He wanted me to teach, and if I dedicated my classrooms to Him, He would anoint them. Inspiration for this belief came from 2 Chronicles 7, which speaks about the dedication of the temple King Solomon built for God. When the dedication for the temple was completed, the glory of the Lord filled it.

I always prayed, no matter where I lived, for the Lord to place me exactly where He meant for me to be and for His presence to fill my classroom. After my first year of teaching, my husband and I moved from Indiana to near Boston, Massachusetts. I was told during my search for a job in one school system that they had over 300 teachers in the area applying for the few jobs available. My situation was somewhat complicated in that my husband was to be in the area only a year and a half as a veterinary intern. I didn't want to deceive anyone about my circumstances, so I always revealed them in interviews.

Still, the Lord gave me favor with the assistant superintendent in one school system. When I called to ask about the status of my application after an interview, I was somehow able to speak directly to him. I told him how much I liked his school system and his response amazed me. He said, "We liked you too, and we have responses from two of your three references. We are waiting on the third one, but I am going to go ahead and offer you the job." I could not believe my ears, but I knew that his offer came from the work of the Lord on my behalf! I was given a one year contract in a wonderful elementary classroom, replacing a teacher who was to be on sabbatical. At the end of the school year, one of the fathers brought me a beautiful framed watercolor he had done in appreciation for my work with his child. Forty years later that painting is still hanging in my home as a reminder of God's gift to me that year.

After my husband completed his internship, we moved to Columbia, Missouri, where he took a position at the University. After the birth of our second child, we decided I should stay home with our two children. When our youngest was almost three years old, a series of events caused me to return to teaching. This decision did not come easily, for I had been selling cosmetics to earn extra income and really did not feel prepared to go back to the classroom. To complicate matters, I had an inner ear disorder that occasionally caused serious episodes of dizziness.

At one of my cosmetic parties, I met a secretary for the superintendent of a school system that was a forty-five minute drive from my home, and I mentioned I had taught sixth grade for four years. She said they really needed some good teachers in their school system, and I asked her to send me an application, believing she would never follow through. Of course, I had numerous reasons why I would not want a teaching position anyway.

A few days later, the application arrived. I decided that although it was not something I really had a desire to do at the time, I would leave it up to the Lord to close this door if this job possibility was not from Him. I completed the application and mailed it, not expecting to hear about it again. It was March and I did not give it any more thought until the first of August.

Then, for the first time in a long time, I began to burn with desire to return to the classroom. My inner ear problem seemed to have gone into remission, but I submitted only one application and that was to the superintendent's secretary of the school system forty-five minutes away.

Two weeks prior to the beginning of a new school year, I received a call from the principal at one of this system's elementary schools. His school had just been informed that they needed to hire one more sixth grade teacher, and he went to the board office and simply pulled out my file from a drawer full of applications. I was hired to teach sixth grade science, but the resources I received left much to be desired. I was given four different sets of textbooks that were over twenty years old and science equipment that fit nicely on just one shelf. However, just as the Lord multiplied the fishes and loaves to feed five thousand people (Matthew 14:15-21), He anointed my classroom and multiplied what was given to me. Out of necessity, I learned to develop my own science lessons based on materials that could usually be found in the kitchens of most homes. I based over thirty years of teaching hands-on science on what I learned in that school.

Just as the Lord multiplied my material resources, He increased what I was able to do with students because He Himself was with me in the classroom. Later, in another school system, I taught middle school science for eight years. Frequently, I was given students who had issues that challenged the classroom management style of most teachers. I certainly didn't have great expertise in handling unruly students, but I was not alone in my classroom. The Lord used one particular student during that period in my life to teach me about the hearts of some students who behave poorly in the classroom. This student kept my attention the entire time he was in my class, and I prayed regularly about how to handle him.

One day as I was giving my students a summary of an activity in which they had used lima beans, I suddenly slipped on some of the beans and fell forward into a chair. The chair then slid across the room with me in it. I fell out of the chair and lay on the floor for a few moments. The students were stunned into complete silence. One student ran from his seat and came rushing to my side to see if I was still among the living. He yelled, "Mrs. C! Mrs. C! Are you all right?" The voice I heard was that of my behavioral problem student. I heard the Lord speak to me in that moment, "This child is in your classroom for a reason." I then felt inspired to collaborate with other teachers in my school to form the "C" team for the purpose of working individually with challenging students like him. The "C" stood for Caring, and every teacher on the team "adopted" one or two struggling students for the purpose of diagnosing their problems and searching for solutions that might bring them some success. The Lord blessed our efforts, and much was accomplished in the hearts of every teacher who became a member of that team

Someone once said, "Days and weeks sometimes go by slowly, but years will just speed by!" I found that to be true as my years in the classroom went by very quickly. A few years ago I became one of the teachers in my generation who retire early and continue to work part-time. The last three years of my career, I was a part-time science coach at an elementary school. The principal of the school was a wonderful, Christian man who actually created the position for me.

When he assigned me a classroom to use, I decided I would anoint every doorway, desk, and table in the room. That room belonged to the greatest teacher who ever lived, Jesus Christ. At the beginning of the school year, I told fellow teachers that I would invite them to bring their classrooms to my room, so I could teach special hands-on science lessons for their students. I was a little nervous about my invitation because my thirty years of teaching experience was with sixth graders, and previously I had not wanted to teach younger students. However, the Lord was the real science teacher, and He gave the invitation from my lips.

The first year in my role as the science coach for the school, I taught every classroom from kindergarten through fifth grade. Teachers would come into my room and warn me about certain students who they feared would misbehave. Every lesson was blessed because I was only the vessel for the "Real Teacher." Only when I prepared to teach my very last class in the building that first year was there a problem. Chaos prevailed throughout the lesson, and when the students left, I could hear the Lord's voice clearly in my spirit. He was saying to me, "I just wanted you to see what it would have been like without Me!"

I asked the Lord during the three years I remained in that position to teach and develop every science lesson I taught. I was continually amazed about my students' excitement over the activities they experienced in my classroom and how much pleasure I received from being with them. There was a very special atmosphere in the room, and it did not come from my talents or expertise.

The Lord always has a plan for our lives, and if we seek His will He will bless our career choices. I know that He blessed all of the days I spent in the classroom and I smile when people say we can't have religion and prayer in our schools today. There is no legislation that can keep the Lord of Moses, Abraham, and Jacob away from the students of a Christian teacher. Jesus Christ is in the body of every believer, and He is the best teacher that ever walked this earth! Wherever Christians go, they take the living God with them.

Philippians 4:13

For I can do everything with the help of Christ who gives me the strength I need.

2 Corinthians 12:7b-9

But to keep me from getting puffed up, I was given a thorn in my flesh, a messenger from Satan to torment me and keep me from getting proud. Three different times I begged the LORD to take it away. Each time he said,"My gracious favor is all you need. My power works best in your weakness." So now I am glad to boast about my weaknesses, so that the power of Christ may work through me.

CHAPTER FIVE

Flight of the Bumblebee

Let Christ Surprise the World through His Work
in You

*M*ike Lee has been deceased now for many years, but the influence he had on the lives of others will last forever. I met Mike in 1974 when I went to the Barrow County School System in Winder, Georgia, as a young teacher. He was the assistant principal at my elementary school, and at that time, I had only four years of teaching experience. I was also an "escapee" from being at home with two young children and having no car to drive while my husband was at work. I was so thrilled to be at school that sometimes I alienated some of the older teachers who were anxiously anticipating retirement.

Some of the stress in those days originated from such responsibilities as maintaining an accurate attendance register for the school year. I can still hear the administrator's words, "Everything entered has to be in ink, and if you fail at this task you may lose your teaching certificate." As all of this was being explained, I had a vision of my teaching certificate being in the process of "going, going, and gone!" Keeping a permanent attendance register in ink was frightening to a young teacher who could never get the lunch money collection to add up correctly. The cost of a student lunch was thirty-five cents, and I was always coming up with the wrong amount for the class total. I repeatedly searched my purse for the correct change to finish the task, so I could begin my lessons each day.

I desperately needed the assurance and confidence from someone like Mike Lee. Without his help I am sure that I would have gone on to another career, and what that would have been is a mystery to me all these years later. Mike was so different from the administrators I had known previously as student and then as teacher. He did not drink coffee as most of us did, but instead he would empty a package of peanuts into a glass bottle of coke and drink it. That was his fix for the day. His great sense of humor made a lot of rough places smooth for many of us. When we dealt with stressful situations related to classroom management, he could always see humor that was invisible at first glance to those around him. Indeed, if anyone became more invested in frustration than was merited, he would say, "Boy that 'so and so' sure gets his pants in a wad!" Just visualizing that made one laugh.

Mike had the powerful gift of making people believe they could accomplish more than they ever dreamed. He demonstrated empowerment long before it became such a popular term in education. It was no accident the Lord put Mike into my life at a time when I was just beginning my career and still had some very idealistic notions about teaching. The Lord knew I would need the inspiration provided by Mike Lee to sustain me over the long teaching career included in His plans.

I would go to Mr. Lee with ideas about creative projects I wanted to implement in my classroom, but I had no clue on how to make them a reality. I had ideas "without legs." Mike would never laugh at my thoughts and he always explained how we could make them happen.

I once told Mike I wanted to do a science fair that was different from the traditional ones held in our school system. It would be a hands-on experience where students came through the fair and actually did activities under the supervision of the students who had set them up. (This was the concept of the popular Scitrek which was located in Atlanta, Georgia, for many years.) I didn't know how to organize such a science fair, but Mike explained to me, "I am sure we can get all the materials you need, and I'll start on it right away." Before I could lose my confidence and change my mind, Mike was aggressively involved in the planning and organizing, and against my better judgment, I was fully committed. His enthusiasm created a momentum of its own, and I could not back out and disappoint him.

In those days there were popular plaques which had the myth of the bumblebee printed on them. The myth is that according to the laws of aerodynamics, the bumblebee has too much body weight and the wrong wing span to fly. The bumblebee, however, does not know this, so he just flies. Mike taught many of us around him to "fly" like the bumblebee.

Of course scientists today have come up with a definitive explanation of how the bumblebee can fly. Isn't it really wonderful that the flying bumblebee never knew about this myth? I think this is a point of inspiration for all Christian believers. Not knowing what you are *not* supposed to be able to do, you "charge ahead" anyway. Walking in faith, you "just do it!" That is what Philippians 4:13 is all about. "I can do all things through Christ who strengthens me."

The world will always have another explanation for unexpected success. People who enjoy explaining these results will tell you why you were able to achieve them after all. I was once told in the seventh grade that I might not be college material. I have always wanted to locate that person and tell him that I earned three college degrees and became a teacher because I believed I was called to this profession. Most of all, I would want that person to know that the reason for my success was the Lord, who enabled me to do whatever was required of me. A friend of mine, who was also an unlikely college student, earned her doctorate claiming Philippians 4:13. She claimed this verse every step of her unlikely journey and later gave a wonderful testimony about what the Lord had done in her life

Mike taught others to fly with the confidence of the bumblebee. He gave teachers the courage to follow their inspirations and teach their students to do likewise. Thousands of students benefited from his talents, humor, and high energy level.

What makes this story even more remarkable is that Mr. Lee suffered so much physically. Having had polio as a child, he was able to walk only with braces on his legs and crutches for support. He inspired everyone who knew him. In Mike's physical weaknesses, his strengths as a person of great personal courage were seen vividly.

One day in my classroom, a student suddenly came up and grabbed me by my arms and immediately began having an epileptic seizure. I shouted for one of the students to go get help. The first person to arrive was Mike Lee, and upon seeing the distressed student, he quickly threw his crutches down and kneeled beside him. The person in the building least physically capable of helping that young man was the most effective person he could have had at his side. It was no accident that, as a young teacher, I saw Jesus in the crippled administrator kneeling at the struggling epileptic student's side. Mike had so much light in him, and that light was contagious to those of us who worked with him. His inspiration remained with me my entire teaching career.

After Mr. Lee died, a math and science resource center I originated with grant money for the school system was dedicated to him. His family also donated money for the center, and some of those funds were used to publish an activity book. Two other teachers and I decided to write this book, which would encourage parents and students to do math and science activities at home and experience the fun of learning together. I have always believed that hands-on science activities are a vehicle for families to discover how spectacular this world is and what a creative giant we have in our living God.

We had dreams of earning a great deal of money for the center and even of being on some television show as successful teacher authors! The book, called *Take out Science and Math to Digest At Home* [3] did not become a best seller. However, it was distributed to several hundred teachers and parents in our school system. In the front of the book was a dedication page to Mike Lee, so everyone who received it might know about this wonderful inspirational human being.

My prayer for all those who dedicate their lives to being educators is that they will be courageous enough to follow the lead of a person like Mike Lee and teach their students to be bold and follow their inspirations.

Regardless of your profession, even if you don't work outside your home, be like the bumblebee! Let your inspirations guide you, do the unexpected, and let the world come up with its own explanation. You will always know the truth and you will have the power of the living God guiding you every step of the way.

Genesis 4:6b-8, 13- 15 *

"Why this tantrum? Why the sulking? If you do well, won't you be accepted? And if you don't do well, sin is lying in wait for you, ready to pounce; it's out to get you, you've got to master it." Cain had words with his brother. They were out in the field; Cain came at Abel his brother and killed him.

Cain said to God, "My punishment is too much. I can't take it! You've thrown me off the land and I can never again face you. I'm a homeless wanderer on Earth and whoever finds me will kill me."

God told him, "No. Anyone who kills Cain will pay for it seven times over." God put a mark on Cain to protect him so that no one who met him would kill him.

Titus 2:11

For the grace of God has been revealed, bringing salvation to all people.

*The Message

Chapter Six

Grace Not Accepted

A Miracle of Choice—Grace Is Ours If We Accept It

I looked over the shoulder of my unhappy student and saw that she had drawn a picture of a witch. She was angry with me and decided to seek revenge with her art work. She labeled her masterpiece *Mrs. Cornelius*. I looked at her and laughed as I said, "I look great!" She couldn't help herself, so she laughed with me! God just interjected His grace into a potentially stressful situation.

What is grace? It is one of the most precious gifts the living God gives to all His people and is His undeserved favor and love. Many times I have seen grace given in places where I did not expect it and in circumstances where I did not recognize it until much later. On many occasions, God has revealed to me this wonderful gift at the level of my most urgent need. There were numerous situations in my many years in the classroom where

God's grace rescued me, and He made His presence known to me.

I have also been a participant in many Bible studies and Sunday school classes where people digressed from the chosen topic and seemed to go in all different directions of thought. I have witnessed the presence of God's grace that remarkably allowed the leader to get everyone back on track so that the intended message was delivered. I have also observed God's grace being expressed in a very tense moment when someone in a group interjected some delicious humor and everyone relaxed. I believe that many times in those kinds of moments, since we are made in God's image, God also laughed.

Moments of grace are present every day, and I hardly pause to notice them, but I certainly dwell on the instances where grace does not come to me. This is most sharply defined for me when sin is the issue. It is one thing to receive grace when I am neutral or likeable, but it is quite another to receive it when I have violated someone and I am guilty of a hurtful or terrible action. Remember the lyrics of the song "Amazing Grace" describe a "wretch *like* me" receiving grace. I know without a doubt when I sing that song, the "wretch" *is* me!

God's grace was on Adam and Eve as He clothed them at the cost of animals' lives, and this sacrifice of the blood used to cover them foretold the cost of covering us with Christ's blood. I will be eternally grateful that the blood of Christ covers my sins.

Sometimes it takes a while to see the profound long-term consequences of sin. So many times we assume when we become disgusted with ourselves that God is also permanently disgusted with us, and we don't realize that God's opinion of us is eternally more favorable than our own. I know I struggle to realize how precious I am to Him.

Andrea Bocelli's song "Because We Believe"[4] includes these words: "Like stars in the sky we were born to shine because we believe." Our fear is that God has put so little potential in us, and that we are totally messing up. The truth is He has put so much of Himself into us that we have the power to be very important to His kingdom's work.

Satan, on the other hand, will do anything to make sure we do not accept God's grace, understand what we are meant to do, and realize how important we are to God. I am so in love with my seven grandchildren, but God's love for them is deeper than any love I could humanly possess. He has that kind of love for all of us, and although it is very difficult to comprehend love of this depth, I know it is true.

Satan will try to convince us that if we are really good people, we will continue to grieve over our sins long past the time of our repenting and God's forgiveness. How many times have I done something, felt convicted of my sin, and then repeatedly asked for forgiveness? Satan encourages us to do this, so the focus is on ourselves instead of the kingdom's work. The Lord asks us to be convicted of our sin and ask for forgiveness, but He does not condemn us. Condemnation comes from Satan to keep us from living victorious lives in the light of the Lord.

Looking at the story of Cain and Abel in Genesis 4:1-16, we can see an important lesson about sin and repentance. Cain did not recognize that God was looking at his heart when he favored his brother over him. Cain could not see that Abel presented his offering to God with a heart of worship. God pursued Cain and talked to him before he killed his brother, but he did not wait long enough for grace to get his attention. He let his impulsiveness and jealousy rule his actions. He did not realize that even after he had chosen evil, he did not have to remain stained by his decision. Satan would have all of us believe that we have no more chances after we have done something horrible. The truth is the Lord will still offer us the opportunity of repentance. There was a mark on Cain so others would know not to kill his body, but the invisible mark on his spirit was possibly the one that caused him the most distress. The mark on his spirit came from not being reconciled with God and receiving His grace. The grace of a deep and true repentance could have changed his life. Instead of being filled with distress and darkness caused by hiding from God's face, life could have been entirely different for him and his family.

How does the story of Cain and Abel relate to Christians today? Surely, most of us don't personally know anyone who has killed his brother; therefore, we cannot comprehend how anyone could do something so horrible.

I want to tell you a story about a little six-year-old girl and her nine-year-old brother. The little girl loved her brother who had been sick for a long time and she prayed for him to be healed. However, jealousy invaded her spirit when she saw that people were always bringing her brother gifts and giving him all their attention. She just blended into the background, or so she thought. When she tried to get her brother to let her play with his new toys, he always told her, "No."

One day upon her brother's refusal to share, she said the most unforgiving thing anyone could ever say to another person: "I wish you were dead." A few months later her brother died, and the little girl was devastated. She was convinced the good child died, and the bad child lived. Unlike Cain, she was repentant, but she couldn't accept God's grace because she could not forgive herself. She knew that she did not kill her brother, yet her words rang loudly in her spirit and there was a condemning mark on it.

As she grew she knew the Lord and understood in her mind that she was forgiven, but the dark mark remained. Whenever hurtful things happened to her, she believed she deserved them, even though her sin was buried deep in her subconscious.

Even with this misery inside of her, she began to see miracles from her prayers and continued to see them all of her life. When she turned twenty years old, she recalled the hidden memory and revealed it to her fiancé. He appealed to her, "You were only six years old when you said those words. It is time to forgive yourself!" She was not ready for self-forgiveness, but she was so relieved that her fiancé could still love her. Her fiancé's encouragement was a step on the road toward her experiencing God's grace.

She loved the Lord, talked to Him, and heard His voice throughout her life until she was almost fifty years old. The Lord had been pursuing her all this time. Finally, she let God's light into her spirit and understood yet another dimension of His grace. It took the Israelites forty years to make a ten day trip in the desert, and it took this woman forty years to accept God's grace which had been immediately offered.

The woman allowed the Lord to remove the mark on her spirit. For the first time since she was six years old, she felt clean and new inside. This gift was offered all those years ago, but she couldn't accept it until she allowed God's spirit not only into her mind, but also into her heart. That is what experiencing God's grace is like. One feels clean and new no matter his age or circumstances. I know this because I was that little girl.

Jesus said that we must enter God's kingdom as a child. There are many facets of being a child of God, but perhaps one of them is having a heart that is innocent, pure, and uncorrupted by the world. The living God's grace can restore our hearts to that of a child's!

Cain never experienced the grace of a deep and true repentance. He could have had the dark mark on his body and spirit removed by God's mercy and grace. I wonder how many people in our families and circle of friends need to experience God's grace in this way. Sometimes there are people whose feelings are hurt far too easily. They are quite critical of others and have very low self-esteem. They can't seem to recognize their own God-given gifts, and they don't believe in themselves. Some of these people know the Lord, but something in their lives causes them not to forgive themselves. I spoke to someone recently who told me my prayers for her had been answered, and for the first time in her life, she could see her beauty as a person. She was glowing as she realized for the first time in her fifty years how God saw her.

We are *all* beautiful in God's eyes. Isn't that amazing? Pray for the people in your life who hurt you or others with their words. They may need healing of the pain that is piercing their spirit. They may not have accepted the miracle gift of God's grace in their lives. They may not know what it is like to lay down the burden of guilt and experience the newness of life that the living God offers. Pray for them and pray for yourself to accept in full measure the grace of God!

BARBARA J. CORNELIUS

Matthew 18:19-20*

"Again I say to you, if two of you agree on earth about anything they ask, it will be done for them by my Father in heaven. For where two or three are gathered in my name, there am I among them."

* English Standard Version

CHAPTER SEVEN

Sisters Rejoined

Sisters Experience Healing through the Power of Prayer

$\mathcal{I}$ would rush home from school with great excitement! I couldn't wait to see my one-year-old baby sister, Sue. She was born when I was five years old, and I loved playing with her. She was so adorable. My eight-year-old brother, Bobby, and I would happily work together to change her diapers. Bobby had been very ill for some time, and this baby brought so much joy into our home. Our family's world fell apart when my brother died at the age of nine. The day of his funeral, this precious now two-year-old toddler waddled into the living room wearing my mother's high-heel shoes, and family members could not help but smile.

My opinion of my baby sister changed when she was about three years old, and she began to get into all my things. Seeing some of my belongings scattered and broken made her no longer so adorable to me. However, my grieving parents doted on her and spoiled her in every way possible. This little girl brought comfort into their crushed, grieving spirits, and she made them smile by just being in our home.

As we grew older, Sue and I were at odds with each other, and I always believed she was jealous of me. I could easily identify all our differences. In my mind I could make a long detailed list of those things that created her jealousy. Since she was only two years old when our brother died, she did not remember him and I did. I earned three college degrees, and she was able to complete only two and a half years of college. My husband and I had more material wealth than she and her husband. We were frequently in conflict with each other, and I had a tremendous amount of anguish because Sue didn't seem to like me. I wanted my sister's love! What I didn't recognize was that I was carrying a superior attitude, and that helped to build a huge barrier between us. My sister and I could not find any common ground as children, and the problem continued into our adult lives.

That is not our story today. Do you want to know what changed our situation? As I prayed for favor with my sister, God pierced my conscience and revealed to me how I viewed myself as the more informed, educated, and superior sister. The Lord let me see that my haughty attitude was creating a wall between us. The truth is that Sue has a special relationship with the Lord, and she is a wonderful supportive wife to her husband, who is a Methodist minister. She has great spiritual wealth and an enlightened relationship with the living God. By laying down my ego and allowing the Lord to convict me of my transgressions, He permitted me to see her strengths as He does.

Several years ago we began to pray together. I remember the first time we prayed before I left after a short visit, and at the urging of the Holy Spirit, I asked Sue if we could pray together. I am so happy I responded to the Lord's nudging, for afterwards I looked at my brother-in-law's face and saw tears in his eyes. He said, "I wish I could do that with my family."

On another occasion, after my mother visited my sister and brother-in-law in Indiana, they drove her to my husband's family home about an hour away so she could travel back to Georgia with us. Sue and I decided we would begin a new tradition. We formed a circle of members of both families and joined hands to pray. Sue said later, "I felt an 'electric charge' go through my hands when we prayed." God's power and grace surged through our spirits when we prayed as a family.

On several occasions Sue and I went to the altar of the empty church where my brother-in-law preached and prayed for our family members as they struggled with personal and health issues. I am convinced that, as we knelt together, Jesus Himself was there kneeling and praying with us. Many, many of our prayer requests have been granted.

My relationship with Sue is not perfect because we still have our basic personalities that sometimes invite conflict. We are, after all, still imperfect human beings. However, prayer completely changed our relationship for the better. We frequently pray on the phone together, and she recently told me, "You are my best friend and advocate." Later, as I remembered our conversation, tears ran down my cheeks. Can you believe what the Lord did for us? I had begged the Lord for favor with my sister, and He had graciously granted my request. Prayer opened the door of our hearts for the Holy Spirit to work.

My sister told me recently that there was an accident at her workplace, and a worker was in danger of losing a couple of fingers. She and a co-worker who spoke very little English went to the bathroom to pray. With great compassion, my sister prayed in English and the young woman prayed in Spanish. I know the living God was pleased with their prayers because the worker did not lose his fingers.

Perhaps we don't pray with family members because we feel that we don't "speak the same language." We see them as being too different in personalities, goals, career choices, interests, etc. We clearly see their faults, but their strengths are blurred somewhere in the background. Ask the Lord to convict you of any attitudes that you have which are creating a barrier between you and the person whose favor you seek.

Why are we so reluctant to put our arms around family

members and pray for them? Who could possibly be a better advocate than a person who loves them? Put aside your petty differences and pray together sincerely and watch the power of the Holy Spirit bind you together and give you favor with each other!

You, too, may rejoin with one or more "lost" family members and have more intimate, rewarding relationships. Pray together and watch the power of the Living God released in your lives. Pray aloud over your husband or wife, child, mother, father, sister-in-law, mother-in-law, or other members of your family. No one can possibly surpass you as their advocate with the living God. He will reward you in ways you might never imagine.

BARBARA J. CORNELIUS

John 1:16-17 *

And from his fullness we have all received, grace upon grace. For the law was given through Moses: grace and truth came through Jesus Christ.

John 11:25

"I am the resurrection and the life. Those who believe in me, even though they die like everyone else, will live again."

* English Standard Version

CHAPTER EIGHT

Hearts Joined by Grace

A Mother-in-law and Daughter-in-law Healed by Grace

$\mathcal{T}$wenty years ago my husband and I were in Indiana visiting his family, and we prepared to leave after a two day visit. We were going to see my sister and her husband, who lived just a couple of hours away. Our plans changed when fog rolled in, and we were not able to leave. I had always told my husband Larry, "I have noticed that when we visit your family, your parents seem to become a little agitated after a couple of days. I think if we want to maintain family harmony, we shouldn't stay longer than that." On this particular visit, it was necessary to stay a third day, which turned out to be very traumatic.

Larry's mother, Vera, and I were both a little restless that day. She and his dad had quit smoking after thirty years, which resulted in emotional and physical suffering for them. Adding to the situation was the fact that I had left the classroom and taken a new position at the board office in my school system. Even though I felt led by the Lord to make this change, it was a very stressful time for me. The first few months in my new job had been quite challenging. Before we could leave, Vera decided to tell me what she really thought about me after twenty-five years of marriage to her son. Her comments reached to the depth of my insecurity and left me with a much wounded spirit. I had thought that if a grading system for daughters-in-law were in place, I had a "B" average. It turned out I was receiving an "F" as a daughter-in-law, and I was too stunned to argue. I did not make a return visit for two years.

Staying away was in direct opposition to my beliefs as a Christian, but I was just too insecure and emotionally injured to return. Finally, after meeting with a counselor, visiting my pastor, and much prayer, I did return. However, I remained cautious around Vera for many years. I was waiting for her to resume her conversation with me about my deficits as her daughter-in-law.

Our situation changed a few years ago, after I experienced spiritual healing. When I felt the newness in my spirit that comes from accepting forgiveness from the Lord, I completely forgave my mother-in-law for her critical outburst and myself for not being a perfect daughter-in-law. Having experienced wonderful healing in my relationship with my sister, I felt inspired to begin praying with Vera when we visited. Also at the urging of the Holy Spirit, I began to pray daily for her. I prayed for any hurt that might be inside her to be healed and for the Lord to bless our relationship. I have found that it is very difficult to be mean-spirited to someone for whom you pray. It is not impossible, but it is difficult! Praying for someone who has hurt you also allows the Lord to heal you.

A few months before Vera died, my husband asked me to assist him and other family members as they moved his mother from her own house into a nursing home. This was a gut-wrenching time for the entire family, and Larry told me, "The two of you have a special connection, and I need you at my side." Would you like to know where that special bond came from? It resulted from God's grace being bestowed on both Vera and me through our prayers for each other while together and when apart. The last time I spoke to Vera on the phone, I prayed for her, and she thanked me for the beautiful prayer.

The final time I visited with her was when I told her goodbye prior to leaving her at the nursing home. We looked into each other's eyes and said a heartfelt, "I love you!", and when I leaned down to kiss Vera, my necklace fell into her face. I "clobbered" her with my necklace! God's grace was there, and we both laughed.

Three months later in the midst of saying goodbye to Vera, the entire family experienced a mountaintop experience. We felt great sorrow, but another dimension of God's grace is that even in suffering the loss of loved ones, He gives the wonderful grace of His presence. In the midst of our pain, He sends us Himself.

We were at the hospital for Vera's last few hours, and she was semiconscious and in much pain. Seeing how restless and agitated she was, we filled the room with God's word. We read praise scripture to her from Psalms and Proverbs. Larry's brother told us that he had sung "Amazing Grace" to her before we arrived, and that led to other family members singing to her. Larry and one of his sisters even sang a song about stepping on carpet tacks. Vera had made up the song when they were children to help distract and comfort Larry after he stepped on a carpet tack. We assured her that Jesus was there with her, and everyone could feel the mood in the room totally change. Vera became much calmer and more peaceful as the Lord poured out His spirit into that hospital room. Many family members who were present spoke about it. We will never forget what the Lord did for all of us that day, as He stood beside us while we told my mother-in-law goodbye.

It was my honor to give the eulogy for my mother-in-law, Vera Cornelius. I had never had an experience like that and felt quite inadequate, but as I sat at a computer and talked to family members, the Holy Spirit composed the eulogy through my fingers. Before the funeral began, I wept as Larry prayed for the Lord to speak the words Himself through my mouth. It was a total victory for the Lord! Larry's family came together spiritually as they never had previously, to say goodbye. God poured out His Spirit on us during the time before, during, and after the funeral. The mountain top experience He provided for us came through the gift of His Grace.

The best gift of grace is yet to come. When our days on this earth are finished, we will have recreated, resurrected bodies, and we will be with our loved ones in heaven. It is God's promise to us! The living God watches over His promises to fulfill them. I look forward to the time when I can see my mother-in-law, Vera Cornelius, again and tell her I love her in the presence of our Lord.

BARBARA J. CORNELIUS

Luke 15:8-10

"Suppose a woman has ten valuable silver coins and loses one. Won't she light a lamp and look in every corner of the house and sweep every nook and cranny until she finds it? And when she finds it, she will call in her friends and neighbors to rejoice with her because she has found her lost coin. In the same way, there is joy in the presence of God's angels when even one sinner repents."

Nehemiah 8:10b

The joy of the Lord is your strength.

CHAPTER NINE

God's Lost and Found Department

Seek God in Prayer for What Is Lost—He is Listening

My father arrived home from umpiring a high school baseball game and was in a very agitated state. He was a beloved high school teacher and thoroughly enjoyed participating in extracurricular activities. He had wonderful rapport with his students and was interested in their lives outside of the classroom. If they had a pressing need in their lives which he knew about, he would provide encouraging words.

Before the baseball game started that day, one of his students approached him and asked a favor of him, "Mr. Spencer, I worked all summer to earn money for my class ring, and I don't want to take any chance of losing it during the game. Will you please keep it for me?" The year was 1956 and money for class rings was hard to come by. My father agreed to take the ring and placed it in his pocket, not giving it another thought. When the game was over, the student asked for his ring, only to see my father reach into his pocket and find nothing but the hole where the ring had slipped through.

My father and the young man searched the baseball field in vain. Arriving home, my father looked at me and my seven-year-old sister and pleaded, "I need for the two of you to get in the car right now. We have got to go back to the ball field. I lost a student's class ring, and I must find it!" I was twelve years old at the time and had just been baptized and confirmed into the Carbon Methodist Church in Indiana. I felt something very special happened between the Lord and me when I made that commitment. I remember the pastor saying that baptism is an outward sign of an inward change. I felt that inward change as a stirring in my spirit that day, and the feeling has been with me ever since. I asked the Lord to show me where the ring was located, and I fervently petitioned Him all the way to the field.

When we arrived my father parked the car in the grassy area next to the field, and I opened my door and looked down to see the ring at my feet! As far as I was concerned, that answered prayer "sealed the deal" between the Lord and me as a prayer team. I never forgot His confirmation that He always hears me when I pray.

Throughout the years, I have felt led to pray for many lost items. Many times I did not locate these things, but when I did, there was always the Holy Spirit to tell me why I found a particular item. The Lord used these experiences to increase my faith and show me I can call upon Him for every need.

On one occasion when I was in my thirties, I decided to have a black and white snapshot of my brother and me made into an eight-by-ten color picture as a gift for my mother. This treasured photograph was taken just a few months before Bobby died. It was taken on a rare day when Bobby felt well enough to be outside, and it showed the two of us smiling broadly and sitting in our old red wagon. I found someone who would reproduce it for a reasonable price, and I then looked for the picture in the place where I always kept it. It was missing! I searched all over the house and even glanced back in the drawer several times where I believed I left it. Finally, I asked the Lord to reveal its location to me to me so my mother would have the comfort of having this picture in her home that Christmas. I looked in the drawer once more and suddenly saw the picture! How could I have missed seeing it before?

On another occasion I lost my wallet after going to a local Wendy's to get sandwiches. When I arrived home, I realized I no longer had my wallet. I had taken it out of my purse before I went inside so I would have fewer things to carry, but I did not remember seeing it after I paid for my food. I anxiously drove back to the restaurant and searched outside with no success. I then went inside and asked if anyone had found it, but no one had. It was beginning to get dark as I dejectedly went out one of the side doors and peered down towards the concrete where a drive-thru customer was preparing to leave. There in the shadows, where I had looked moments ago without success, was my wallet! Even though some time had passed, no one had seen it and picked it up, and my money and all my important documents were still in the wallet.

In both these experiences, I could not see the missing items in my first attempt, but they were there all the time. I could hear the message that was being given to me by the Holy Spirit, "Many times you pray and search for some desire of your heart, and then decide I am not answering you. All the time, My dear child, the answer is in front of you. Pray for 'spiritual eyesight' so that you can see it."

A different time, I lost a citrine stone from a favorite ring. The setting was a very soft gold and did not firmly grasp the gem. The mesh gold was beautiful but the stone was very inexpensive, so I had not bothered to have it reset. I really enjoyed the ring and was disappointed when I lost the citrine. I searched several times over the next eight months, and one day I found it under a small refrigerator in my classroom. I actually lost it on several more occasions and each time I gave up hope, the stone would reappear. The message was clear: I should not let my mind dictate *when* I should give up hope for a prayer request. I finally lost the stone one last time, but I believe that I had been allowed to keep it for many years so the Holy Spirit could teach me about faith and hearing God's voice.

My most memorable experience of finding a missing item occurred after the funeral of one of my former sixth grade students who died in a biking accident during his seventh grade school year. He jumped off a high ramp without a helmet and fell face first onto the concrete; he died almost instantly. He was his family's only child and grandchild. His best friend, another former sixth grade student of mine, was there with him when he died. This young man not only kept his composure, but he comforted his friend's mother as she knelt beside her dead son. I never attended a more emotional funeral and never felt closer to the Lord as I cried out for His comfort to be provided for the family as they dealt with their heart-breaking loss.

I wore a gold necklace with a garnet heart to my former student's funeral. This necklace was very special to me, because my husband had given it to me. Larry was never very much into gift-giving and the fact that he took time to purchase something special for me made it a treasured piece of jewelry. I was home from the funeral for a few minutes when I attempted to remove my necklace only to find that it was missing! I found the garnet heart that had been on the necklace near a closet door and realized that the necklace must have fallen off in my bedroom. I looked all over the bedroom many times and searched the entire house to no avail. Finally, after turning on all the lamps and overhead light, I got down on my hands and knees and slowly felt every square inch of the carpet in my bedroom. The gold necklace was not to be found. When I was about to give up searching, I looked across the room to the area in front of my dresser and there, shimmering in the light, was the necklace! There was no missing the gold as it glowed in the light. How could I have not seen or felt it? I could hear the Lord saying to me in a silent, but very clear voice, "Many times you *look* for Me and do not *see* or *feel* My presence. Not only am I there with you in those times, but My presence is as shiny and glistening as the gold necklace." Wow!

I prayed with great emotion for the family who had lost their beloved son. I was told that they were unable to have any more children, but even so, I prayed that the Lord would give them a child. Knowing that the son who died could not be replaced, I still prayed for the comfort of another child for the lonely parents' aching arms. Two years later against long odds, they had a baby boy. Amazingly, the family of the friend who had been with the young son as he died also experienced a miracle. This family had two boys, and they also thought they were unable to have more children. About the same time, the Lord gave them a baby girl. The God of all comfort put babies in the arms of both sets of parents.

A few years ago another former student, who was in her early thirties, lost her much older husband to suicide. My heart always went out to her since she had suffered a broken engagement a few weeks before her scheduled wedding. Later she did marry but now suffered this crushing blow. My heart ached for her losing her husband in such a horrible way. The Holy Spirit directed my spirit to pray that the Lord would give her a husband to love her and a child, if that was her heart's desire. A few months later she married a young man and later had a baby. After her baby was born, a friend of the family said, "I have never seen anyone who wanted a baby as much as she did!"

Recently, she told me, "Stop praying so hard! I am already expecting my second child." It was not my praying that returned her joy and gave her a precious family. It was the Lord writing prayers on the hearts of all her friends and family and their lifting them up to Him that delivered her joy and magnified it many times over!

Joy can be wrenched out of our hearts. Joy can be lost. Our hearts will ache, and our heads will tell us that what was lost can never be found again. That is a lie from the enemy. The truth is that the Lord is in charge of the most important "lost and found" department there ever was. He can retrieve lost joy, lost happy family relationships, and lost souls. Nehemiah 8:10 says "Don't be dejected and sad, for the joy of the Lord is your strength!" We were meant to have joy in our spirits and in our lives as we walk with the Lord. He is there to provide it whenever it seems lost forever, and He is always there at our side whether or not we see or feel His presence.

Jeremiah 1:4-5

The LORD gave me a message. He said, "I knew you before I formed you in your mother's womb. Before you were born I set you apart and appointed you as my spokesman to the world."

Isaiah 49:5

And now the LORD speaks—he who formed me in my mother's womb to be his servant, who commissioned me to bring his people of Israel back to him. The LORD has honored me, and my Lord has given me strength.

CHAPTER TEN

The Young Prayer Warrior

Miracle of a Premature Baby

$\mathcal{I}$ sat in the labor and delivery waiting room sobbing. My husband and I were called to the hospital because my daughter was in premature labor. She had been ill and her sickness made it difficult to detect that she was in labor, and her baby was not due for almost seven weeks. When she arrived at the hospital, she was too far along for her doctor to attempt to stop the natural process. Indeed, it had all gone very quickly. She had been at the hospital for about an hour and she was about to deliver her baby.

I was filled with fear that she was going to lose this precious little boy named Brandon. The entire family fell in love with this baby as soon as we knew she was carrying him. It is so difficult to explain to others how you can love someone you have never seen except on an ultrasound machine! Her obstetrician took time to comfort me before my husband and I were asked to leave her side. He reassured me that everything was going to be fine. "He'll be small, but he will be all right." he said.

After several minutes, my son-in-law came into the waiting room and excitedly told us, "He is here!" He told us that the doctor said we should be able to see him in a couple of hours. Those couple of hours expanded to nearly eight. We became more and more anxious as time crawled by without any new information.

Finally, we were told that the medical team was trying to stabilize Brandon and had almost lost him a few times. His lungs were not well developed, and he actually had the same condition as President Kennedy's baby when he died a few days after his birth in 1963. Even though this was 1997, we were fearful that the same thing would happen to our precious grandson.

The prognosis was guarded, but we were asked if we wanted to see him. I just knew that if I could see and touch him, the Lord would surely save Brandon as He touched him through my fingers. I believed that the Lord could save this baby without my help, but I was convinced that I was supposed to be at Brandon's side as I prayed for him. I knew that my prayers would be magnified if I could touch his tiny foot as I pleaded for God's healing power to enter his body. Before I left this newborn, I prayed for the Lord to send His angels to watch over him.

That night after we arrived home, my husband and I called all our family and friends who are prayer warriors, and within a few hours Brandon was put on prayer chains all over the country. Hundreds of people were lifting him up. My extreme terror of losing this dear child was gone before I went to bed, and it was replaced with absolute peace.

When I called the hospital the next morning, I talked to one of the pediatric nurses and she told me, "He made it through the night." Almost daily for two weeks my husband and I went to the hospital to see this tiny four-pound baby. I was so thankful that Larry was a veterinarian and board-certified in small animal internal medicine. He would always ask specific medical questions, and the answers we received felt like soft rain falling on my spirit. This information made the fear of the unknown disappear.

It was so moving to see this tiny baby on a ventilator for so many days, struggling to keep his place in the world. We were told not to touch him after the first couple of days because it agitated him and brought too much physical distress. We celebrated when, at one week, he was taken off the ventilator, and every day thereafter were steps forward and steps backward.

I prayed daily for God's angels to surround Brandon and protect him. Some angels were humans with nurses' uniforms, and I could see the power in them given by the living God as they spoke to us. After two weeks, we began to feel God's assurance that we were going to be able to keep him. We knew that God had done much to protect Brandon and that we were all on a journey that was going to bring honor and glory to the Lord's name.

When Brandon was about one month old, Larry and I were allowed to hold him. I was so excited, but I was also more than a little nervous to maneuver all the cords around so that I could hold this cherished treasure in my arms. As Brandon's days in the hospital continued, I, along with other family members, would go visit him. I would change his diaper and do anything I could, so I could touch him and pour love into his spirit. Someone once told me that a baby was too small to understand the words "I love you!", but I know those words are comprehended by the spirit. It is a language translated by the Holy Spirit for all who carry Christ in their being.

Finally, after six weeks in the hospital, Brandon went home with his parents. He was sent home on a breathing monitor that would sound an alarm when he momentarily stopped breathing. Many times in the hospital the alarm would go off and the nurses would change his position to stabilize him. I was so thankful for the nurse who assisted me the first time this happened in the hospital while I was holding him. I sometimes wonder if alarms like that go off in heaven when danger is lurking for God's people, and angels then go into action to make sure we don't leave earth before our missions are completed. I know angels were there with Brandon the entire time he was in the hospital, and I also know they followed him home.

After being home for about three weeks, Brandon developed a problem which became another medical crisis. He began to experience projectile vomiting and was taken to Egleston Children's Hospital in Atlanta, Georgia. The diagnosis was pyloric stenosis (blocked stomach outlet), which required immediate surgery. This little baby on a respiratory monitor was going to be anesthetized and have surgery.

I remember wondering how this could be happening as I questioned the doctors and reminded them of Brandon's circumstances. They were very understanding and told me how many times a week they performed this same surgery on small children. Even though they were experts in their profession, I knew who the Master Physician was and still is. Along with other family members, I appealed to Him to do the surgery Himself through the surgeon's hands. Jesus is the Master Healer, and He would be in the operating room. On Christmas Eve, Brandon went home in time to be with his grateful family as they celebrated their first Christmas with him. God's timing is perfect!

This special child and his mother came to live with us when he was around one year old because his parents decided to divorce. God gave my husband and me the opportunity to guard over this wonderful treasure and support our daughter, Jennifer, as her life went down an unexpected path. Every night when we put Brandon to bed, we prayed over him. When he awoke during the night crying, we were there to comfort him and make him feel secure. We were God's hands on him, and the Lord was at our side directing our steps. We will always carry in our hearts those memories from the year and a half he and Jennifer stayed with us.

When Brandon was about seven years old, we asked who would like to offer a prayer at the restaurant where we were having lunch. He volunteered, and as I heard his prayer, I was astounded! This little boy prayed like an adult who had been a prayer warrior for the Lord for many years. He prayed much like Samuel of the Old Testament must have prayed as a child. How could he have so much of the Lord's spirit in him at such a tender age? I believe as he was formed in the womb, he knew the presence of the Lord.

Brandon amazes all of us with his spiritual eyes. At the age of eight, Brandon told me to look at the sky as we were traveling toward our church. He said, "I see a cross in the sky!" After parking the car, I looked upward expecting to have to search the skies for the image he was talking about. I was amazed to see a huge cross in the sky above me.

This happened soon after the movie *The Passion of Christ* [5] was released. My husband and I saw it, and a few of our friends questioned the commercialism that surrounded its release. Personally I will never forget the vivid message of that movie. It is so like our Lord to get our attention through a child, and it is no accident that the Lord let Brandon see His cross. I shared this observation with others as I witnessed about the message I received by watching the movie.

Later that year, Brandon took the microphone at one of our church luncheons. He proceeded to tell the one hundred people in attendance that he had prayed for several years to have a daddy in his home and that God had answered his prayers with his new stepfather. He proudly pointed his finger at our daughter's husband of a few months. He gave a witness for our Lord that I am sure made Him smile in heaven!

When Brandon was nine years old, he decided he had had enough winters without any snow. That January he prayed that the Lord would send him some. Sure enough, one Wednesday evening as we were preparing to leave our church after the fellowship activities were finished, we saw something unexpected happening outside. Huge snowflakes were falling from the sky, and as we carefully made our way home, we were fascinated with the white winter wonderland that was surrounding us. "Praise the Lord!" Brandon shouted all the way home. The Lord had not been able to resist showing His glory to His child.

As of this writing Brandon is twelve years old and is in middle school. He has enriched the lives of our entire family. He has his struggles and challenges us to use our spiritual reserves when his battles become that of conquering his emotions. When he talks about the teasing he receives from other children, I tell him that sometimes the Lord sets us apart from others to make sure that we hear His voice and follow His path.

It hurts when we don't excel at things of our choosing that would help us feel accepted by our peers. It puts sorrow into our spirit when others call us names and speak to us as if we are not worthy. Worldly discouragement is offered in huge doses by Satan to make sure that we do not advance God's kingdom. I know that is what I experienced as a child. Today though, I know what marvelous things the Lord did with the pain in my spirit, and I praise Him for doing so!

Brandon's middle name is David, and he certainly has a heart that reminds me of King David of the Old Testament. Brandon has offered comfort to people who have life-threatening diseases, and he has prayed for their families to encourage them. I continue to marvel at what the Lord has done as I watch Brandon grow physically and develop intellectually and spiritually. I frequently talk to the Lord and ask Him, "Did you notice what precious thing my grandson has just done? Did you see the bubbles he just blew? Did you see the pictures he just drew? Did you hear the song he just played on the piano?" Does the Lord Almighty know what His miracle has meant to me and my entire family? Of course He knows and sees these things because He is omniscient, but I have a profound need to bless the living God with my expressions of joy about what He does. I will never forget what He has done for Brandon and our family. Never!

My prophecy for my grandson Brandon is that he will inspire many people to become part of God's kingdom during his long life. His childhood struggles will make him a person of faith, conviction and courage. He will strive to bring comfort to others, for he knows the pain of a wounded spirit. He will bring great honor to the Lord and pass God's light to many generations.

For all the remaining days my husband, Larry, and I have on this earth, we will cover Brandon with prayer. When we are called home to be with the Lord, we will continue to celebrate the gift of our grandson and delight in seeing him bring honor to the Lord's name.

Walk in faith when you walk through the valleys of your life because the Lord is at your side. Remember to praise the living God for the beautiful moments you witness in the lives of your loved ones, and cover them daily with your prayers, that they may bring honor to His name.

A Prayer for My Child/Grandchild
By Barbara Cornelius

Dear Heavenly Father,

I praise Your Holy Name and welcome you into my family's lives today. I give thanks to You for giving me my family and allowing me to experience real prosperity as my loved ones make imprints on my heart.

I pray for favor and influence with my child that he/she may see You inside me. Increase the light of Your Holy Spirit in me that I may become contagious and affect my child's vision of the world.

Please surround my child with warring angels today to protect him/her against the darkness of this world, physical harm, and lies that might be told to him/her about himself/herself.

Pierce his/her conscience when he/she makes comments that are framed by the absence of respect, truth, and love.

Anoint his/her mouth and ears that he/she may bring honor to Your Name today and hear the music that you put inside of him/her.

Give him/her a clean heart that he/she may see clearly Your Kingdom's work for the day ahead. Give him/her a pure heart that he/she may see You and recognize Your voice.

Give me wisdom and faith that I might quench the fiery darts of the evil one, as he attempts to bring disharmony and strife to my home through my child's weaknesses.

Bless my child that the inner light You placed inside of him/her will be so bright that a thousand generations will be blessed because of his/her walking with You.

In the name and power of Jesus Christ, I declare this prayer for my child.

Amen.

72

BARBARA J. CORNELIUS

Philippians 4:13 *

I can do all things through Christ who strengthens me.

Psalm 23:3

He renews my strength. He guides me along right paths, bringing honor to his name.

Isaiah 43:19

"For I am about to do a brand-new thing. See, I have already begun! Do you not see it? I will make a pathway through the wilderness for my people to come home. I will create rivers for them in the desert!"

* New King James Version

CHAPTER ELEVEN

The Red Silk Dress

God Cares About Everything We Do

I had not sewn anything for many years, and here I was trying to craft a red silk dress for my eight-year-old grand-daughter, Alyssa, for Christmas. Experiencing some frustration, I remembered my sewing experiences from twenty-five years ago. I was not very accomplished all those years ago, but I had been motivated to sew for my young daughter, Jennifer. I wanted her to have a pretty, long dress for Christmas. At that time there was very little to choose from in the stores, and this was many years before all of the shopping opportunities had materialized on the internet. I had decided to use what few skills I had and ask the Lord to help me sew dresses for my little girl. Of course Jesus, the "Master Carpenter" is also the "Master Tailor," and I knew He would answer my prayer!

I began sewing for Jennifer when she was just over a year old. Not having any previous instruction, I struggled greatly as I tried to make some sense out of dress patterns and the instructions that came with them. I remember ripping out many sewing projects because I was slow to understand how the pieces fit together. One of my first efforts was a long dress and bonnet. I even made a matching outfit for my daughter's doll. My handiwork was poor, but the pictures of my little girl in her dresses were wonderful. Every year until Jennifer was ten years old, I made her a Christmas dress.

I also made dresses for a friend's daughter who lived several hundred miles away. We became great friends when our sons were a year old. We had been pregnant at the same time with our daughters, and we both cried when my family moved away. Our daughters were not quite a year old when we left, and my friend and I were so disappointed that we were not going to see them grow up together.

I prayed over the dresses as I made them for the two girls. Although I didn't have exact measurements for my friend's daughter, the dresses always fit. Sewing those outfits gave me opportunities to see what the Lord could do with "willing hands." I learned that the Lord is definitely in the "sewing business" because He is interested in everything we do. My faith grew with each dress I finished. This gift of faith helped to prepare me to trust Him many years later when trials and tribulations threatened the well-being of my family.

My husband and I were given the opportunity to walk together in faith when Jennifer moved home with her precious little boy after she and her husband separated. I will never forget when she told us that she was pregnant again. The timing in the middle of the separation from her husband was not perfect for human calendars, but it was totally perfect on God's calendar. The first words out of my mouth were filled with joy as I said, "Maybe God will give me a granddaughter."

Jennifer made five trips to the emergency room when she was pregnant with Alyssa. I went with her each time and prayed,

"Lord, please allow us to keep this wonderful gift, and let this child not be born until she can be completely whole." Experiencing the Lord's guidance with complicated sewing patterns that were confusing to me all those years ago taught me to trust the Lord in situations that made no sense. Alyssa is the only grandchild of my seven grandchildren whose birth I witnessed, and I was there to hold her a few minutes after she was born. It was love at first sight! I will always feel that the two of us have a special connection which goes beyond any logical explanation because of that experience. It was simply one of the best days of my life.

My husband, Larry, drove us to the hospital the morning Alyssa was born and stayed in the waiting room with her other grandmother. They both held her when she was a few minutes old and remarked about how beautiful she was. Although my daughter and Alyssa's father were not together, he arrived at the hospital when she was one hour old and held her like he was holding a million dollars in his arms.

I still remember vividly the drive home from the hospital with our newborn granddaughter. We took Alyssa into the house and lovingly placed her in a new white baby bed. In preparation for her arrival, I had painted her room with a fresh coat of white paint and put up a border of male and female rabbits dressed as little boys and girls. Happiness permeated our home in the middle of a crisis for our daughter. God had blessed us in an unexpected way and carried us through a rough patch in our lives!

When this wonderful baby girl was only a few months old, we could see these very "old and wise" eyes looking back at us. Surely Alyssa must have spent much time with angels before she was born. She has always shown maturity and wisdom well beyond her years. Even though she is almost two years younger than her brother, she is usually the one that looks after him and reminds him of where his misplaced clothing and toys are located. The older I get, the more I realize that I need the same kind of assistance from this beloved child, and God truly smiled on me the day she was born.

Alyssa has always loved to dance, sing, and twirl her baton. Certainly, she was born with music in her spirit. At the age of less than two years, she would sing along with the songs of her favorite television programs. She delighted the entire family with her "ABC's," "Twinkle, Twinkle Little Star," and "Rock-a-Bye Baby." There were many times when this dear child lifted her single mother's spirit as she struggled to raise two little ones by herself. She gave her brother needed support and security that only the living God could have prepared when planning for her birth. Only He knew that two-year-old Brandon needed the love and connection that a baby sister named Alyssa would provide. Only He knew what a blessing she could be to our entire family!

As Alyssa grew, she fell in love with all the things little girls like and which grandmothers like to provide. For years clothing purchases had to be pink and glittery. There were never enough dolls, strollers, toy sinks and dishes. When she took ballet for a few years, her glamorous, graceful side was accented. I was so relieved that she had not inherited my clumsiness and lack of poise.

When Alyssa was five years old her mother, Jennifer, remarried. The Lord had sent my daughter a wonderful young man. I am sure that at the same time he was falling in love with my daughter, he was falling in love with his future step-daughter, my Alyssa. Never was there a quicker, more loving bond formed between step-daughter and step-father. If her biological father had not still been an important part of her life, I am sure her stepfather would have adopted her. She became the daughter of his heart, and there has never been a more protective and loving step-father. It became very easy for her to call this man "daddy."

At the age of eight, my granddaughter no longer loved pink and instead preferred dresses that were a little more grown up. So here I was attempting to sew a red silk dress for Alyssa. My cousin, who owns a fabric store and is an excellent seamstress, had already assisted me with the crafting of the matching purse for the dress.

When I began cutting out the pattern pieces for my granddaughter's dress, I realized that I had forgotten almost everything I learned all those years ago. God knew I could not possibly make this dress without His hand upon me and my sewing machine! I remember when I was Alyssa's age, and my maternal grandmother made dresses and matching purses for my cousin and me. Although we cannot find any pictures of these dresses, the expression of love from a beloved grandmother remains in my spirit today. I prayed Philippians 4:13 over and over as I worked on Alyssa's dress, growing in confidence the Lord was doing something new in me that would be seen by my granddaughter.

When Alyssa's dress was finished, I took her to a photography studio to have her picture taken. She looked absolutely beautiful in the dress, and she glowed as she received many compliments about her appearance. We also had a picture taken of me proudly standing beside her in her new dress. These photographs are memorial stones for the family, and I believe that future generations will look at these pictures and know that the message is "Look what God can do!" This message was given a deeper meaning when Alyssa wore her dress to church for the first time.

That Sunday became memorable in ways I had not expected. Alyssa decided to have hot chocolate, which was served between services in the fellowship hall. When I saw the hot chocolate, I reminded her to be very careful and not get any on her new dress. Moments later, she accidentally spilled the contents of her cup on her dress and matching purse, which was lying on a nearby table. My mind was racing with anxiety, but I calmly went to the kitchen and retrieved a wet towel to wipe off as much of the hot chocolate as I possibly could. The purse had become a sponge and soaked up much of the spill. In a few minutes the dress, which had been full of huge, wet spots, had dried. Then the surprise came! You could no longer see the stains on the dress, and even the purse still looked beautiful. I asked Alyssa what lesson she learned from this and with bright, shiny eyes she said, "God cleaned up my dress!" At the age of eight she was learning what it took me decades to learn. Our sins make stains on our lives, but God came to take them away and make us clean and new as if the stains were never there.

The following year when Alyssa was nine years old, after selecting her own pattern and fabric, she made her own red Christmas dress with assistance from me. Perhaps, when Alyssa marries and becomes a mother, she will fashion clothing for her children. My prayer for her is that she will sew not only dresses but also sow seeds for God's kingdom. May she walk in faith all of her life and trust God to do new things in her life which will be a tremendous witness to her children and grandchildren.

I believe everything we do with our children, grandchildren, and others provide us with new opportunities to bring honor to the Lord's name. Remember to lay down memorial stones for generations that will follow you and let every person see what God can do through us when we walk with trust and faith!

James 5:13-15 *

Are you hurting? Pray. Do you feel great? Sing. Are you sick? Call the church leaders together to pray and anoint you with oil in the name of the Master, believing prayer will heal you, and Jesus will put you on your feet. And if you've sinned, you'll be forgiven- healed inside and out.

Psalm 92:4

You thrill me, LORD, with all you have done for me! I sing for joy because of what you have done.

2 Chronicles 20:21-22

After consulting the leaders of the people, the king appointed singers to walk ahead of the army, singing to the LORD and praising him for his holy splendor. This is what they sang: "Give thanks to the LORD; his faithful love endures forever!" At the moment they began to sing and give praise, the LORD caused the armies of Ammon, Moab, and Mount Seir to start fighting among themselves.

* The Message

CHAPTER TWELVE

Daughter Reclaimed by the Hand of God

God Thrilled Our Souls with Our Daughter's Miracle Healing

$\mathcal{W}$e were traveling from our vacation at the beach as rapidly as the speed limit would allow on that fateful morning when my cell phone rang. We had ended our vacation a day early because the night before we had received a call from our pregnant daughter telling us she was ill and was going to see her doctor. Our son-in-law, Earl, spoke in a hurried, anxious voice as he told us, "They are going to take the baby. They don't know what is wrong with Jennifer!" A few minutes later, another family member called on my cell phone and said, "A heart specialist and a lung specialist are with Jennifer. They are delivering the baby in a few minutes." We immediately knew that Jennifer was in the midst of a mighty struggle for her life. The news sent shock waves throughout our bodies, and we braced ourselves for what lay ahead. I cried softly, and my loving husband reached over to hold my hand.

Our daughter had remarried several months previously, and her new husband did not have children. With his wonderful, caring heart, he claimed our daughter's son and daughter as his own. Jennifer and Earl decided to have a baby to add to their happy family, and she had no difficulty getting pregnant.

The first several months were uneventful, and despite the fact that our daughter's first child was born six and a half weeks early, this pregnancy seemed to being going perfectly. One day at school, almost seven weeks from her due date, she began to feel ill and left her third grade classroom to go the office for help. She noticed her nail beds had turned blue, and her body began to shake violently. Even her voice began to vibrate with the shaking.

Her assistant principal entered the office and upon seeing Jennifer, realized that she needed to call the EMTs immediately. The paramedics came and examined her and said they could find nothing wrong with her that was serious enough to require medical attention. Clueless about the cause of her physical state, one of them asked, "Have you been stressed or anxious about anything lately?" After they left, she called her husband to come and take her home. Checking in with her obstetrician and discovering he was not in his office to examine her, they headed to the hospital. After she arrived they hooked her up to a monitor to assess the baby's condition. Finding nothing wrong with the baby, they sent her home and recommended she contact her family doctor.

After remaining at home for another day, she experienced excruciating pain in her chest. She commented later that she could not remember feeling this uncomfortable in her entire life. Later that night, Jennifer and her husband went to the emergency room. Again, the doctor could not find anything wrong with the baby, and he suggested she should return home.

Normally a very agreeable and cooperative person, my daughter refused to go home. Finally, after being in the emergency room for three hours, a wonderful Christian doctor examined her with a stethoscope and detected what none of the other physicians had heard. She immediately sent her to have a chest x-ray. The problem that had been missed for the last two days was not with the baby but with the mother.

The x-ray revealed that Jennifer had pneumonia, and she had developed pleuritis, an inflammation of the lining of the lungs that is very painful. In a few hours the pain was so severe they gave her morphine.

We received the call at our vacation house that morning telling us that she was very ill, and we immediately packed our car and headed home. We knew it would take six hours to reach our daughter, and those would be very long hours. As we headed helplessly down the highway, we received phone calls that alerted us to the fact that our daughter's life was hanging in the balance.

We called every prayer warrior we had the presence of mind to identify. As the tears flowed, we prayed and talked to family members by phone. As the calls were made, our prayer request for our daughter went on prayer chains around the country.

The trauma for our daughter was two-fold. The baby began to show signs of stress and needed to be delivered immediately, and if our daughter were to survive, medications potentially harmful to the baby needed to be given. The race against time to save two lives began in earnest.

We arrived about two hours after the baby was delivered by cesarean section in the emergency room. It was of great comfort that our pastor, visiting in the hospital at the time, had arrived in time to pray with our daughter before her baby was delivered. As we looked back later, we realized our pastor's being in the hospital at just the perfect time was God's planning.

We found our daughter in intensive care, breathing with the assistance of a ventilator, and mostly unaware of what was happening around her. Miraculously, the baby, even though she was taken several weeks early, was doing great. She was a healthy baby and after a few weeks would probably be sent home. She was on a ventilator for only a few hours.

My husband and I waited anxiously until we were allowed

into our daughter's room. We went into the darkened room and held each other's hands and wept as we saw our daughter at the edge of a cliff with death waiting at the bottom. We were not in that room alone. As we began to pray aloud for the living God to come to her rescue and bring healing into her body, we felt His presence at our side. I am sure that her room was filled with angels. I remembered that when she was a sleeping baby, I summoned them to come and guard over her. I am certain that some of the angels guarding over her in her present crisis were the same angels.

Christian friends from all over the city where we lived came to the hospital to pray with us. During the hours we waited, we stood in a circle in the intensive care waiting area and prayed aloud with people from her school, our church, and even with her ex-in-laws. This area was open to the entire hospital with many, many people passing by as they made their way to other areas of the hospital. I cannot even imagine who the Lord witnessed to that night. We will probably never know everyone affected until someday when we meet in heaven.

We had friends who were attending a four day Christian conference ("Walk to Emmaus") who later told us they had prayed all night and raised their shields of faith to extinguish the fiery darts Satan was sending towards our daughter. My sister-in-law, Lana, in Indiana said later, "I sang praise music and prayed all night for Jennifer." She had done just what the Israelites had done hundreds of years ago before they marched into a battle that would bring them victory through their faith in the living God! (2 Chronicles 20: 21-22).

We later learned that when Jennifer's doctors delivered the baby, they believed our daughter might be only a few hours from death. Her obstetrician told us, "After looking at the x-rays and CT scans, we determined that her lungs were two-thirds solid with the appearance of cream cheese. It was clear only a miracle could save her."

Finally around two o'clock in the morning, I encouraged her husband and other family members to return home for the night and let me stay in the waiting area to watch over her. Throughout the night I went into her room in intensive care and prayed for her and pleaded with the living God to reclaim her life from that cliff of death.

The next day we saw remarkable improvement and her obstetrician smiled as he left her room. After three days the ventilator was removed and she left intensive care for a regular hospital room. Progress was slow as fluid built up around her lungs.

Jennifer went through the painful procedure of having a large amount of this fluid removed. Even though she was only seven years old when her Grandfather Spencer died, she said that she felt his presence in the room when she was suffering from the pain of the large needle going into her chest. It was over twenty-five years since she remembered being in my father's presence, and there he was with her in her time of crisis. The living God goes to great lengths to provide us comfort when we most need it.

After a week in the hospital, our daughter was not making any more progress, and it was unknown when she might leave the hospital. Our friend Joseph from Ghana arrived with our son, Jeff, to pray with Jennifer. He anointed her with oil and prayed for her healing to be completed.

Afterwards, Joseph spoke with Jeff and me outside of Jennifer's room. He said, "Satan tested your faith, and he has failed in his attempt to destroy it. It is now over for the evil one!" He then joined hands with us and prayed with us, and afterward he gave us the prophecy that in three days our victory would be complete. Joseph made his prophecy on a Tuesday, and by the following Friday, our daughter turned the corner and improved so rapidly that she went home on Saturday. She was in the hospital for twelve days, and her beautiful baby girl, Jacie Evelyn, went home several days later.

God gave me my daughter at her birth. Now, He let me, as well as her entire family, reclaim her at the birth of her third child. Just as my story was not meant to end when I was almost killed in a car accident many years ago (Chapter 2), my daughter's story in God's kingdom was not yet finished.

The Lord God gave us comforters every step of the way. He gave us the Holy Spirit to pray with us as we made our way to the hospital. He stayed with us while we were at Jennifer's side in intensive care. He gave us friends at the hospital to pray aloud with us as the Holy Spirit spoke to our spirits. He gave us a prophet from Africa to encourage us and give us a witness to healing that would be complete. He blessed us with the spiritual presence of a family member who long ago left this earth. No matter what transpires in the rest of my life, I will never, ever forget what God did for our family! Never! May the witness in this story bring great glory to the most Almighty and Precious Living God.

Whenever you go into "battle", remember to praise the living God. There is nothing He will not do, according to His divine will, for those who believe and act in faith. Always praise His Holy Name and let Him know when He has thrilled your soul. Praise Him in all things and let Him know that you love Him for who He is! We were born to praise the living God.

Psalm 8:3-5 *

When I look at your heavens, the work of your fingers, the moon and the stars, which you have set in place, what is man that you are mindful of him, and the son of man that you care for him? Yet you have made him a little lower than the heavenly beings and crowned him with glory and honor.

Ephesians 6:14

Stand firm then, with the belt of truth buckled around your waist, with the breastplate of righteousness in place.

* English Standard Version

CHAPTER THIRTEEN

Mean Words

Don't Play Satan's Game of Hurtful Self-Talk

*T*he agitated first-year teacher stood next to me in my classroom and said, "I hate to tell you this, but the expensive video tape you loaned me is stuck in the VCR, and I'm not sure I'll be able to get it out without destroying the tape!" As he was speaking, I remembered the golden days of my early teaching career when I broke a large reel of movie film as I attempted to thread it through an old projector. You cannot imagine the mess I made of that movie.

I know this young man did not expect the reaction he received. I laughed and told him, "If you teach school for a hundred years, you will not be able to match me in similar disasters I created in my thirty years of teaching! Many people have bailed me out along the way, so don't worry; if the tape is ruined, I will replace

91

it." To his great relief, the tape was successfully ejected later in the day.

I have suffered in my life from many "senior moments," uncoordinated acts of movement, "foot in mouth disease," and from decisions based on plain old stupidity. I don't want to be an overachiever in my quest to document my point, but describing a few examples will probably enable many people to sigh with relief and acknowledge that their bad moments were never as bad as mine.

On one occasion when my son was about three years old, I attended a morning meeting with other young mothers. Sitting in my next door neighbor's kitchen, I asked the other women, "Does anyone know where my son is?" I had lost track of him in all the confusion of several women and children.

The answer of one of the ladies was shocking. "Barbara, he is sitting in your lap!" Mercifully, there was little discussion all those years ago about Alzheimer's disease showing up in thirty year old women. This recollection has been my reference point over the years when I consider whether or not my memory is becoming worse as I age.

I have misplaced the same objects over and over—especially car keys—and accomplished regular cleaning and organizing of cabinets, drawers, and closets in my search for lost articles. Somehow, all this activity gave me a positive mindset instead of a feeling of resignation to an act of futility. I do like to turn my faults inside out and find a strength hidden somewhere in the murkiness. As a messy teacher in the midst of coworkers with clean and neat desks, I frequently said, "A really messy and disorganized desk is a sign of genius!" Somewhere I saw a poster stating that little nugget of wisdom and realized it worked for me by changing my weakness into a strength.

I once drove my car along a muddy road to see a new house that was being constructed in my neighborhood. It was difficult explaining to my husband and family why I thought that it was so important to see that house since the expedition required a tractor to pull our mud-caked vehicle to safety. My children will never let me live that experience down!

I have always taken pride in my appearance, and I love to shop for stylish clothes and accessories. However, I am a person who occasionally "wears her food," and I have noticed over the years that it is a family trait. In all the years I taught school, I had cleaning supplies handy for the occasions when I spilled something on my outfit and didn't want to spend the day looking like I did not possess any clean clothes.

God does have a sense of humor about us human beings. He demonstrates that when He lets us experience moments where others can join in the fun at our expense. It keeps us humble; that is for sure! One day when I was in a leadership position in a school system, I visited a middle school science class wearing one of my favorite pants suits. I even stopped in the bathroom before my entrance to check my makeup and overall appearance. I had been in the classroom only a couple of minutes when I could hear some of the students laughing quietly. The teacher, who was a good friend of mine, approached me with a big smile as she pulled a foot long strand of toilet paper from the back of my tailored pants! Later, as I shared the experience with other teachers, I spoke with great insight when I said, "This incident surely made some of the insecure middle school students who witnessed my attire feel better about *their* embarrassing moments!" It took some effort for me to turn this incident inside out to protect my feelings.

Difficulty with not being able to remember friends' and acquaintances' names has caused me some of the most embarrassing moments during my lifetime. It does not matter if I have known someone for thirty years or thirty seconds. If called upon to retrieve his or her name, I will have temporary amnesia and possess little hope for recovery. I might be able to call someone by her own name one minute, and the next minute I would address her by someone else's name. On one occasion I tried to introduce my brother-in-law of several years to a friend and could not remember his name. Another time, I introduced a friend of over thirty years by the wrong first name to a church group.

I told her to stand so the group could wish her happy birthday. I didn't understand why she didn't acknowledge me, but finally, over the laughter of the group, someone corrected me and gave her proper name.

I have also experienced many uncoordinated moments in my life, not only with my speech, but also with my physical movements. Several years ago in my classroom, I had difficulty pulling down the screen that was mounted above my chalk board. I must have pulled a little too vigorously because the screen flew off its mounting and knocked down the classroom clock above it and everything else in its path! Recently, as I rushed to board a bus that was headed to the stadium on my way to a nighttime university football game, I fell face first onto the concrete right next to the bus! I am sure the attendant thought I was dead as he dropped his walkie-talkie and picked up my broken eyeglasses. I quickly gathered up all of my belongings and hurried onto the bus, and fortunately I did not break anything but my glasses and my fragile pride. My team won the game and I would have fallen again the next week if that would have resulted in a win instead of a loss.

I have hundreds of moments in my life that have kept me from thinking too highly of myself as I demonstrated many of my physical and mental weaknesses. For many years, I responded by silently calling myself "stupid," "idiot," "unworthy," "clumsy," and similar adjectives. I addressed myself with any mean word I could come up with quickly. My self-esteem was always on the line, and I mistakenly identified low self-esteem with humility.

The problem with addressing yourself frequently with condemnation is that it causes tremendous emotional pain that consumes you and diminishes your power for victorious living. It keeps you from being outwardly-directed, which is just where Satan wants you to be! Condemnation leads to defeat, but conviction of sin leads to repentance and restoration. Ephesians 6:14-17 tells of the importance of putting on our "armor" daily. Verse 14 describes putting on the "belt of truth." It is important to do this to protect yourself from lies and errors you tell yourself or others tell you about yourself.

Even some of God's mightiest people have moments of dwelling on their insecurities and losing focus of who they are because of God's power in them. They also do a little self-deprecating name calling.

After Elijah (1 Kings 18:16-40) went head-to-head with the 450 prophets of Baal, he had a battle with his own insecurity. Elijah saw the power and might of the living God as He destroyed all Baal's prophets. Yet, he ran in fear when he heard that Jezebel, King Ahab's wife, intended to kill him. He mistakenly believed that he was the only prophet for God who remained alive, and he even prayed to die because he was so afraid. He said he had had enough and was no better than his ancestors. We can only speculate on all the mean words he spoke to himself.

The Lord sent an angel to restore Elijah physically and spiritually. Then the living God demonstrated to Elijah that He was not in a powerful wind, earthquake, or fire. He showed him that He was in a gentle whisper (1 Kings 19:1-12).

That is how the Lord speaks to us today. He does not put us on the "receiving line" of powerful, defeating soul condemnation. Guilt will cause us to tell ourselves that we are the worst of the worst and probably the only person who has ever experienced a particular condition. Mean words that rob us of our self-worth and dignity are not God's words. The living God calls us to the conviction of our sins and then offers us the grace of a true and deep repentance. We are so precious to Him, that He sacrificed His only Son for us. He worries we will not know our place in His kingdom as His children who are born again to new lives of victory.

Satan will try to convince you of the lie that if you really are repentant and have no arrogance, you will not forgive yourself of your sins and should "hammer yourself" over and over with guilt. Your barrage of insults against yourself will be endless if you accept this lie.

The truth is that Christ came to bring us freedom and redemption. Accepting conviction and repentance means we accept the sacrifice of Christ's life for us. By doing so, we take back the power we have handed over to Satan and regain the dignity God meant for us to have as His precious children.

Denounce mean words when they come into your thoughts, and declare victory over the evil one! Then all the negative energy you have spent on defeat in the past is replaced with victorious living and knowing who you really are in God's kingdom.

BARBARA J. CORNELIUS

Matthew 25:14-15, 29*

"For the kingdom of heaven is like a man traveling to a far country, who called his own servants and delivered his goods to them. And to one he gave five talents, to another two, and to another one, to each according to his own ability, and immediately he went on a journey.

For to everyone who has, more will be given, and he will have abundance, but from him who does not have, even what he has will be taken away."

*New King James Version

CHAPTER FOURTEEN

The Gift

It Is Never Too Late To Discover and Use God-Given Gifts

I remember a particular sad story as it was told in a sermon given many years ago at my church. The message pierced my spirit, and I never forgot it. A new arrival at heaven's entrance is walking with Jesus and keeps passing unopened gifts. One after another, she passes the beautifully-wrapped packages and finally asks, "Why have they not been opened?"

The Lord sadly tells her, "Those were the gifts I offered you on earth, but you failed to accept them and open them for My kingdom's work." This story always makes me ponder which gifts I might discover I had not opened when I reach heaven.

I also wonder if I had any gifts I opened but tossed aside because of my mistaken belief that they were not really of any consequence to my life and to the world. Gifts can indeed be forgotten as well as lay undiscovered.

My husband, Larry, has the gift of a beautiful voice, and for a few years when he was a college student, he was part of a trio of singers. The trio sang for small groups across the campus of Purdue University, and although it was just a hobby, they enjoyed their experiences immensely. After we were married, my husband and his friends graduated and went their separate ways. For some reason Larry just stopped singing.

On one occasion before we were married, Larry sent me a cassette tape with a couple of his songs, and I loved hearing his music so much that I played the tape over and over. Unfortunately, in a few years the tape disappeared and I no longer had any opportunities to hear my husband's music. Over the years I wished that somehow I could hear his beautiful singing voice again. Sometimes I would stand next to him at church and strain to hear him as he sang softly with the congregation.

Almost forty years went by, and my husband's gift seemed to have disappeared. Then he attended a Christian conference called "Walk to Emmaus" in Indiana, and our lives were touched in a beautiful, profound way. This three day spiritual retreat sponsored by the Methodist Church had been a valuable renewal experience for many of our family members. Larry's sister, brother, and their families had been leaders in the Christian community where they lived and had witnessed to others about the discovery of a new life in Jesus Christ.

My sixty-year-old husband came back from his "Walk" a different man. He was new in Christ! I cried as he told me, "I had it in me all these years, and you kept me close to God." I had prayed for Larry for over thirty years, and by God's grace those prayers had kept him connected with the Lord. Larry was baptized and joined our church that he had sporadically attended for almost twenty-five years.

Later I suggested to him that he should consider joining our church choir because the choir desperately needed more male voices. His answer was very sad to hear, "I can no longer sing. My singing days are over." I spoke to someone in our Sunday school class who was in the choir, and I told her about Larry's singing experience in college. She promptly invited him to join the choir, but he gave her a flat "No" for an answer.

Not giving up that easily, I challenged another friend in our Sunday school class, who also sang in the choir. I told her, "Larry has a beautiful voice, and you need to 'pray' him into the choir." Later, when she encouraged him, he simply stopped saying, "No" and said, "Yes."

At first he struggled with the music. He enjoyed the songs, but felt that he didn't have enough voice left to do the music justice. When he purchased a karaoke machine and began practicing regularly with accompaniment tracks, his situation changed.

One day he suddenly declared, "My voice is back!" Two years after joining the choir, he sang publicly for the first time in over forty years. He sang at a church service with our daughter, who also has a wonderful voice. It was his Mother's Day gift to me, to his mother, on what turned out to be her last Mother's Day, and to a good friend of ours whose husband had just died.

A few months later, Larry sang his first solo at two of the services at our church. These performances led to his singing solo at senior citizen meetings, nursing homes, and even funerals. The Lord had given Larry a ministry of music.

The tape that was lost all those years ago was replaced by a CD of several of his songs. A few months before his mother passed away, we reluctantly placed her in a nursing home, and as she walked into her room for the first time, a CD of his music was playing for her. She lay down on the bed and began to sing along softly.

Later, when a group came to the nursing home to sing hymns, Larry's mother sang along. Someone commented on what a beautiful voice she had. I never heard my mother-in-law sing, and I will always believe that when she heard her son singing, it inspired her to begin singing songs that were hidden within her. Three months later at her funeral, three of Larry's songs that she heard on his CD in the nursing home were played. The witness of his music touched everyone attending the funeral.

Larry's voice continually improved the more he sang. Our twelve-year-old grandson listened to a CD his grandfather made early on and one of his later CDs. He remarked that his grandfather's voice was very good on the earlier CD, but that it was great on his new CD!

Larry later gave our son a CD of his music. He and his wife decided this music would be played for their little two-year-daughter every night when she went to bed. Soon, she began to ask for her "peepaw's voice" when they put her to bed. Frequently, she would sing along as she listened.

A few months later my son arranged a trip for my ninety-year-old mother to her original hometown in Indiana. He took his entire family: wife, two-year-old daughter, and seven-month-old son, and me, on this trip. He said, "I should be the one to make the trip happen for my grandmother because I have a heart to do it for her. I want to give my grandmother perhaps her final opportunity to see friends, family, and the Carbon Methodist Church." My mother had attended this church the entire forty years of her marriage to my father.

The sermon on the Sunday we attended was based on the parable of the nobleman who gave three servants money (talents) to manage (Matthew 25: 14-30). The pastor had given people in the congregation ten dollars to invest and grow for the church's work. As individuals began to share what they had done with the money, I felt a need to witness about another kind of talent.

I grew up and married Larry in that church, and I felt such gratitude as I sat in the pew with three other generations of my family. Inspired to speak, I told the congregation, "My husband had a gift of music that was silent for almost forty years and is now blessing many people in our community. You might also possess some gifts yourselves which are not being used, but it is never too late for the Lord to renew you and use those gifts."

My son stood in the back of the church videotaping the service, and his voice broke and became so soft I could barely hear him as he said, "My daughter goes to sleep every night listening to my father's voice."

Larry's gift is even more precious to his family in that he was almost killed a few months before he discovered his voice had returned. A trash truck with a huge dumpster turned off the bypass too quickly and the dumpster landed a few feet away from his car. Had it landed on his car, he probably would have been crushed to death. God saved him, and his family will always be eternally grateful. We will never stop praising the Lord for the angels that surrounded Larry that day.

Seeing Larry's gift unfold and develop reminds me of the analogy some have made comparing the creation of the world with the performance of a symphony. I once saw a movie about a little boy who goes on a long, painful journey to claim his gift. In the movie "August Rush,"[6] an eleven-year-old boy is waiting at an orphanage for his parents to find him and take him home. His journey to find his parents is paralleled with his finding an outlet for the music in him. Indeed, he hears music in everything around him--in street noises, wind rushing through a field, and in the rhythm of tools being used in a street.

The children in the orphanage where he has lived all of his life tease him and make fun of him. They label him as a freak and treat him as an outcast. He eventually runs away from the institution to look for the parents he has never met. He meets some homeless children and gradually begins to transfer the music in his head to playing musical instruments. Even though he has no musical training whatsoever, he begins composing his own music. He eventually writes a symphony, and at the end of the movie he is conducting a symphony orchestra. You see, he had a special gift that the world did not seem to recognize or appreciate. When he externalized the music that was inside of him, he blessed thousands of people.

I believe Satan will do anything he can to stop us from realizing what our gifts are and what they can mean to God's kingdom. Some people are like Larry in that they have gifts that lie quietly inside them for many years. Larry's gift was the ability to sing beautiful songs. For others, that gift might be the ability to lead a Bible study, to encourage people who have lost confidence in themselves, or to comfort others who spend their days in emotional pain. It might be the talent for some to author a book, and for others, it might be the ability to make people laugh (humor can be so healing). By His grace God has placed gifts in every person, but if one does not open and use his gifts, the living God's earthly "symphony" will be diminished in His kingdom.

The friend who prayed Larry into the choir told me recently how sad it was that his voice was silent all those years. I told her that I believed that his voice coming alive after such a long time was part of God's plan. Larry's story is a wonderful witness to all people that it is never too late for our Heavenly Father to do something miraculous in us at any stage of our lives. We may have forgotten gifts that are dormant inside of us for many years, or gifts that remain unopened but that can still be used for His kingdom's work.

I have never written a Christian book before this one, but this chapter is being written after I have celebrated my sixty-fourth birthday. Thirty-four years ago I led a Bible study in our home, and now I am leading my second Bible study at my church. My husband's witness has touched my life, and I pray that thousands of people will be moved by it for God's kingdom.

Pray to find the "music" inside you and become part of the living God's symphony. No matter your age, it is never too late to renew talents from a previous season in your life and even recognize new gifts hidden inside of you. Ask the Lord to use your gifts to bring honor and glory to Him and His kingdom.

BARBARA J. CORNELIUS

Joshua 4:4-7

So, Joshua called together the twelve men and told them "Go into the middle of the Jordan, in front of the Ark of the LORD your God. Each of you must pick up one stone and carry it out on your shoulder--twelve stones in all, one for each of the twelve tribes.

We will use these stones to build a memorial. In the future, your children will ask, 'What do theses stones mean to you?' Then you can tell them, 'They remind us that the Jordan River stopped flowing when the Ark of the LORD's covenant went across.' These stones will stand as a permanent memorial among the people of Israel."

Chapter Fifteen

Memorial Stones

Remembering God's Answered Prayers

$\mathcal{W}$e stood in the foyer and held hands in prayer for the first time in thirty years of friendship. The four of us attended the same church, went to the same functions at the university, and enjoyed each other's friendship in many ways. Jo Ellen even rescued me from losing a part-time middle school teaching position one school year. It appeared that scheduling conflicts were going to make it impossible for me to keep the position but Jo Ellen eliminated the problem by sharing the position with me. Larry and John had been colleagues and great friends for many years and had played hundreds of rounds of golf together.

John was ill for about four months, and even though a diagnosis of terminal disease was not given, he was wasting away. No physician could seem to get a firm handle on what was causing him to lose so much weight and strength. Unfortunately, we had to cancel our planned trip to the beach that summer, for John simply was not able to go.

Jo Ellen and I frequently walked together in our neighborhood, and we always shared what was on our hearts on those days. After one of our walks, at the urging of the Holy Spirit, I asked if I could come into the house with her and pray aloud for John. I always had a tremendous amount of respect and love for John and Jo Ellen, but I had never before felt led to pray aloud with them. Many times we Christians are very private about our faith, and we tell ourselves that we certainly don't want to embarrass someone by sharing our beliefs.

My feelings about praying aloud with my friends had begun to change in a dramatic way when I called John on the way home from one of our beach trips a few years previously. We left suddenly because we had received the message that our pregnant daughter had been taken to the hospital with pneumonia and was in danger of dying (Chapter 12). John was one of the friends I had called requesting urgent prayer. Later, John stunned me by saying, "After you called that day, I immediately stopped what I was doing and began praying throughout the day for Jennifer to be healed." In all our years of friendship, I had never heard him share anything that personal.

We experienced a miracle for our daughter, and I know that John's prayers were lifted up with those of many other Christian friends. God sent forth His Spirit and roused hearts, uniting them and raising a full canopy of prayer and intercession for Jennifer. God's power was released with each person praying. Now John needed help from his friends, and remembering the magnificent way the Lord answered the prayers for our daughter, I told Larry, "We must go to John's home, and the four of us need to pray together for his healing." There is no prayer chain as powerful as that of family and friends joining hands and praying aloud for one another. All four of us spoke audibly to the Lord that day.

Six months later, we all spent a wonderful, relaxing week

at the beach. The weather cooperated with our plans, and John and Larry returned to our condominium each day with tired but happy faces. They accomplished something they had not done any time before, as they were able to play six consecutive days on the nearby golf courses! The Lord drenched our spirits with joy throughout the week.

On the last day of our vacation, the Holy Spirit reminded me of the story of the Israelites crossing the Jordan River at flood stage. Upon arriving safely on the other side, they laid out memorial stones so that the miracle of what the living God did for them would always be recalled by their children and future generations (Joshua 4:4-7).

I shared this story with the others and said, "The four of us need to symbolically do the same thing and praise God for what He did for us this week!" With all of us in agreement, we sat in the dining room of our vacation condominium and offered a prayer of praise to God. The following week in our Sunday school class, I recounted our experience and urged others to lay out memorial stones for family and friends by sharing with them the great things God has done. Recording these answered prayers for future generations will insure that they will also be blessed by the accounting of what God did. The faith of these generations will be magnified by the witness left behind for them!

So many opportunities to bless future generations are lost because we do not lay down memorial stones for them. I accidentally found one myself a few weeks ago when I went through an old family album. There, in the midst of pictures of my maternal grandmother, was a copy of her obituary which recounted her teaching an adult Sunday school class that frequently had seventy-five to one hundred attendees. It was over thirty years since her death, and I was thrilled to know about her witness for the Lord. I was surprised with my mother's response when I shared this information with her, for she said, "I never knew about it." In that moment, we were both blessed by a loved one who had left a heritage for us so many years before.

Keep a journal or some sort of recording of your faith experiences. Remind family members of answered prayers, and remember to praise God daily for who He is and what He has done! The living God is omnipotent and all powerful, but we can still delight Him by telling Him how awesome and wonderful He is! Lay down memorial stones and let the light that He placed in you be passed to all your future generations!

BARBARA J. CORNELIUS

Jeremiah 1:5 *

"Before I shaped you in the womb, I knew all about you. Before you saw the light of day, I had holy plans for you: A prophet to the nations- that's what I had in mind for you."

James 1:18

In his goodness he chose to make us his own children by giving us his true word. And we, out of all creation, became his choice possession.

*The Message

CHAPTER SIXTEEN

Story of the Promised Son

God Always Keeps His Word

I was twelve years old when I heard the prophecy from the Lord resonate in my spirit, "You will have a son and he will know Me. Indeed, when I was 24 years old, my husband Larry and I were blessed with the birth of our son Jeff. It was such a thrill to have that treasured baby boy become a part of our lives. I was sure that I won the lottery of life's most special gifts.

In my life I have experienced many incidents where I did not pass the tests that daily living provides for a Christian witness. Recognizing that one of the personal qualities I lacked was patience, I asked the Lord, "Please make me a patient person." Honestly, I just expected to miraculously receive the gift of patience. However, as Jeff grew I had many opportunities to acquire this desired trait. He challenged me on many fronts, and I fought to keep him close to me and the Lord.

Satan looked continually for opportunities to place my son and me on "opposing teams." I worked diligently to remind Jeff that we were on the same side. When he was sixteen years old, he told me he was going to wait another year before taking his driving test. Seeing the insecurity that was framing his countenance, I told him, "I won't allow you to *not* believe in yourself! You are going to take that test and pass it." And he did. When Jeff was seventeen years old, I bought the only vehicle I ever purchased in my life without any assistance from my husband or anyone else. My husband told me, "If you want our son to have a new pickup truck, you need to purchase it yourself." So I did, and in doing so, I passed my own test of self-confidence.

During Jeff's childhood, his wounds, whether physical or emotional, were like arrows piercing my spirit. When he was four years old, he fell and tripped on a piece of metal protruding from his sister's baby bed at my parents' home and cut a gash on his chin. His grandparents and I took him to the emergency room, and stitches were required to sew up the laceration. My mother and father held his little hands and tried to comfort him as he screamed in pain. I stood outside the room and sobbed. Seeing him in pain was more than I could bear, and this remembrance of my son's experience causes me to wonder how the living God was able to endure seeing His own Son's suffering on the cross.

I felt my son's hurts intensely, and I was quite defensive about his trials and tribulations. Perhaps seeing the suffering and death of my nine year old brother made me extremely apprehensive about my son's suffering (Chapters 3 and 6). I remember feeling some relief when my son passed his tenth year.

When Jeff was twelve he spent the entire year repairing a go-cart we had purchased for him. When he finally completed all his work and took it for a "spin" around our yard, a neighbor came out and said he needed to stop immediately! It seems that at six o'clock in the evening she was taking a nap and could not tolerate the noise. It took all my composure not to pulverize her verbally. How dare she take his victory away from him! I was more upset than Jeff. Again, I was offered another lesson about my need for patience.

Jeff was always close to my father, and his birth seemed to take away some of the heartache my father experienced when my brother died. I will never forget the first time my father held my three-week-old son. His eyes filled with tears as he cradled his long-awaited grandson. During one visit he held baby Jeff and gave him a bottle while he spoke to a men's group. I sat in the audience fearful of what surprises my baby might provide for his grandfather during the speech, but my father was too full of joy over this little boy to have any of the same fears.

Through the years my father bragged about his grandson to all his friends. He loved to talk to his "precious little grandson" on the phone from his home 500 miles away, and Jeff referred to his grandfather as his "gold." My father died when Jeff was only eleven years old. My son could not bear to go to the funeral home, and he said, "I don't want to see people 'release all the water' they have consumed during the day!" He couldn't handle the pain of seeing the tears of others for his beloved grandfather. My son has the expressive speech of his grandfather and a heart like mine, and he needed to mourn in his own way.

Jeff remained his own person as he grew. One winter day before boarding the school bus, he put socks on his hands because he couldn't find his gloves. At first I was upset with his decision, but then I realized that this choice revealed that it was unlikely that peer pressure would ever cause him to try drugs, alcohol, or anything that would endanger his life.

During Jeff's adolescent years, the Lord kept him separate from the world and the temptations of his peers by giving him a probing, searching personality and short physical stature. He was teased continually by his classmates as they saw that he was different from them, and they sought to exert their power of harassment over his spirit.

Jeff grew to average height by the end of his high school years, and I am sure that his slow growth was part of the Lord's plan for him. I will always believe the Lord used Jeff's painful experiences to separate him from the world and protect him as he navigated life's journey.

I prayed for opportunities to witness to my son, but I feared he would grow up not knowing who he was in God's Kingdom. Once when Jeff was a teenager, he came home from a visit to Six Flags Over Georgia without his new and very expensive glasses. They fell off during one of the rides, and he had unsuccessfully looked for them. We were all concerned about the expense of replacing the glasses. All my life the Lord used missing objects to speak to me and remind me that He was the all-time expert at finding the lost. Now He was presenting me with the opportunity to share this message with my son.

I prayed over the missing glasses and called the lost and found department at Six Flags. The Lord gave me favor with the attendant, and surprisingly he told me, "No, they aren't here, but I will personally go to the ride where your son lost his glasses and look for them." After I hung up, I prayed fervently for the Lord to show this man where the glasses were located.

Several minutes later, the phone rang and we received the news that Jeff's glasses had been found. I immediately turned to my son and told him, "I prayed for the Lord to show this man where your glasses were, and He has given you an important message. Remember the Lord cares about every detail of your life." I knew that this experience would always be a memorial stone for my son's life.

After Jeff graduated from high school, he stopped attending church, and I could not detect his having any interest in knowing the Lord. He stayed away from church for many years, and I kept asking the Lord, "Did I really receive a prophecy from You that I would have a son who would know You?" My hopes and dreams for my son rested with the Lord, and I covered Jeff in fervent prayer as only an adoring mother could. I chose to believe the Lord's promise. I was certain that someday I would see what the Lord saw before my son was even conceived. The Lord encouraged me with the gift of enduring faith.

When Jeff reached his early thirties, I saw a change in him. I was thrilled when a friend told me that she attended an evening church service and saw Jeff go to the altar. What the Lord promised was beginning to be seen and realized. The seeds planted in my son's spirit as he grew and matured began to bear fruit for God's kingdom.

As he approached his thirty-fourth birthday, he became engaged to a young woman who was a friend of his cousin's wife. They were introduced one weekend when he visited our family in our home state of Indiana. Even though we lived in Georgia, Jeff made frequent trips to see this young woman, and after several months, they announced their wedding plans. I knew I should be thrilled about my son's chance for happiness because I had fervently prayed for a wife of the Lord's choosing for him. However, something troubled me about this relationship, but I didn't know what it was. I prayed that if this young woman was not the Lord's choice for my son, He would intervene and would somehow prevent them from marrying.

Six weeks before the wedding, his fiancée broke the engagement. Jeff was devastated beyond any possible comfort that could be provided by his family and friends. He would come over to our house and talk to me for hours about why this had happened. His crushed spirit could not make any sense of this situation, and as I sought to comfort my son, my spirit ached for him. I prayed with my whole being that the Lord would comfort him and send him a wife of His choosing. I would take my son's hands in mine and pray aloud to the Lord to ease his pain and give him healing. Here we were, mother and son, praying aloud regularly for the first time in our lives. The Lord was at work in both our lives to prepare us for His kingdom's work.

During one of his visits, Jeff stood at our front door preparing to leave, and with great sadness in his voice said to me, "I am dedicated to being single for the rest of my life. After the heartbreak I have experienced, I know I will never be married!"

As I received those anguished words, the Lord gave me a message in my spirit for my son and I told him, "Not only will you be married, you will someday have a son! Although I don't know who your wife will be, I can feel her presence so strongly, it is as if she were standing next to me." I had prayed for the Lord to give my son words of comfort, and he used me to deliver them.

A short time later, a Christian friend at church told me that he knew a wonderful young Christian woman named Julie who would be a perfect match for Jeff. He said that this young woman was dedicated to the single life, and it would be the Lord Himself who would have to make this match.

Almost a year after the broken engagement, the Lord started putting my son and this young woman together. Car problems, transportation needed for Christian outings, and similar circumstances seemed to result in them being in the same places at the same times. They were long-time members of our church, but this simply had not happened before.

Before they even had their first date, our friend Joseph gave a prophecy that Jeff and Julie would marry. He even told me to go ahead and choose my dress for their wedding. I certainly listened to Joseph and had a tremendous amount of respect for his words, particularly because I believe the Lord sent him to mentor my son. An adult man often needs someone besides his mother and father to strengthen him and witness to him.

On the day that Jeff and Julie were married, I made an early morning trip to my friend Gloria's house to have my hair done. When I looked at the sky, I saw that it was ablaze with orange and red lights. I could see a city in those beautiful colors, and I could hear the Holy Spirit saying to me in my spirit, "You are seeing a vision of the Holy City that will be revealed when the Lord comes again." Wow!

The wedding took place on the exact day of my husband's and my thirty-ninth wedding anniversary, and my glimpse of the glory of the Holy City was a wonderful confirmation from the Lord that He was blessing this new marriage. Jeff gave Julie a new diamond in the ring set that Larry and I used to exchange our vows all those years ago.

Today my son and his wife have a beautiful daughter and two adorable little boys, and our family will never forget what the Lord did for him. The Lord drenched our entire family in blessings.

Jeff is a tremendous witness to many people in his walk with the Lord. He once encouraged a member of his prayer group to witness to a family member who was fighting drug addiction. He stood tall for the Lord and became a modern Paul as he spoke boldly about the power of the Christian witness of family members to each other. The empowerment of the person he spoke to led to the drug-addicted relative participating in a rehabilitation program.

My prayer for my son is that he will not only stay the course his entire life, but that he will bring many, many people to the Lord. He has a heart for God's work and sees the inner needs of others that are not recognized by most. Jeff is called by the Lord to be a spokesman for His kingdom.

Pray daily with your children and let them see you bring honor to the living God. Pray for the Lord's light placed inside them to increase and be passed to many generations. Lay down spiritual footprints for your children so that they may also do so for their children and grandchildren.

A Family Prayer

Dear Heavenly Father,

Track down every member of our extended family and bring into captivity their every thought, so they will have a heart to belong to You. Breathe on each of them and place Your healing power inside them, releasing them from any brokenness and pain that is suffocating their spirit. Let everyone in our family line be so filled with Your love that they pass Your light to a thousand generations! Let every generation of our family have people who share Your Word, Your Truth, and Your Way!

Amen

Exodus 20: 6 "I lavish unfailing love for a thousand generations on those who love me and obey my commands."

A Family Prayer at Thanksgiving

Ruth 1:1-5

In the days when the judges ruled in Israel, a man from Bethlehem in Judah left the country because of a severe famine. He took his wife and two sons and went to live in the country of Moab. The man's name was Elimelech, and his wife was Naomi. Their two sons were Mahlon and Kilion. They were Ephrathites from Bethlehem in the land of Judah. During their stay in Moab, Elimelech died and Naomi was left with her two sons. The two sons married Moabite women. One married a woman named Orpah, and the other a woman named Ruth. But about ten years later, both Mahlon and Kilion died. This left Naomi alone, without her husband or sons.

CHAPTER SEVENTEEN

Dead End Streets: God's Specialty

When Things Seem Hopeless—God is Just Getting Started

*H*ave you ever been stuck on a dead-end street with no easy way to turn around and go back? Years ago when my husband and I moved to Georgia from Missouri, he drove a U-Haul truck carrying our furniture and belongings. We started out with my following the truck in our car, but after a few hours, the car broke down and we had to tow it the rest of the way. We had our eight-month-old baby, four-year-old son, and the twelve-year-old daughter a friend graciously sent with us to help with the little ones. We all ended up in the front seat of the truck.

The one situation my husband tried to avoid was going down a dead-end street that would require him to turn around. I remember our getting in some difficult places that caused much stress, but we were not traveling alone. We were covered with the

123

prayers of our friends and felt divine assistance that was blessing us.

Sometimes in our life experiences, situations become so difficult we believe there is no way out and that nothing will happen to change our circumstances. Emotionally, we see ourselves at the end of a dead-end street, and with a deep longing for immediate relief we pray for God's help. However, in the process of waiting, we become impatient, and yet sometimes God is saying, "I am doing something here. Wait for Me! You are going to like My solution." Waiting patiently is not a strength that many of us possess, and we just can't look at our plight with the belief that more time will bring about a wonderful answer to our prayers. We struggle mightily, because God's thoughts are not our thoughts, and His timing is frequently different from ours!

One of the most inspiring stories showing God's grace at a dead-end street comes from the Book of Ruth. It provides insight for people who have ever felt they were at the end of the road with nowhere to turn, and it also demonstrates clearly that dead-end streets are God's specialty!

The story of Ruth took place during a terrible time of famine and hardship for Israel when many people were not focused on God and simply did whatever seemed right in their own eyes. Facing starvation, Naomi's family left their home in Bethlehem and went to Moab where conditions were better. The decision to go there had to be heart-wrenching because the Moabites had been their enemies for many generations. Naomi's husband died, and ten years after marrying Moabite women, her two sons also perished. No children were born to her sons, and so it appeared that her family line had ended. However, God did something unexpected for her and her daughters-in-law. He gave them great favor with each other. Naomi, knowing that she and her daughters-in-law had no way of supporting themselves, surely felt that she was on a dead-end street and told them to return to their families. One daughter-in-law, Orpah, reluctantly left, but Ruth refused to abandon her.

When Naomi and Ruth went back to Israel, they met a

relative named Boaz. Boaz was a descendant of the former prostitute, Rahab, who surely must have felt at one point in her life that she had no future. She answered God's call to hide two Hebrew spies sent to Jericho by Joshua and became a part of the victory over Jericho for God's people. Rahab, Naomi, and Ruth are connected in this story because of seemingly hopeless situations they faced which gave them no reason to hope for a joyous answer. Still, God wove their stories together to provide a glorious outcome.

Boaz married Ruth and announced his intention to maintain her dead husband's name and his inheritance, and in time they had a child. The baby was seen as someone to carry on the family line, thus restoring life to a line that seemed to be extinguished with the death of Naomi's two sons. Ruth was the great-grandmother of David. Not only did God extend Naomi's family line through Boaz, He blessed that same family line with the birth of His Son Jesus Christ. God used that love to knit together a future for them and all the generations that followed.

Many women today have had different experiences as mothers-in-law and daughters-in-law and are amazed at the story of Ruth and Naomi. I have always marveled at the devotion of Ruth to Naomi. I could never imagine any human being other than my husband loving me the way Ruth loved Naomi. She was obviously a very special young woman.

Have you ever met someone like Ruth? I have. A few years ago my son believed that he was on his own dead-end-street in his hopes to be married and have a family (Chapter 16). Unknown to him at that time, God was weaving his future to include a wonderful young woman. God is a terrific matchmaker! The story of Ruth and Boaz certainly shows that to be true.

Several years ago, I had the audacity to tell the Lord how much I would love to have this young woman, Julie, as my daughter-in-law. Today, against all odds, Julie is my daughter-in-law. I praise God for her. This young woman has impressed me for years with her devotion to the Lord, and I have never met anyone that has a heart as pure as hers. Julie is always attentive to the needs and concerns of those around her. I have seen her kneel in a pew during a church service to pray with no awareness of anyone around her. Her witness has a profound influence on my walk with the Lord, and she makes me want to be a better person.

Throughout the Bible we see that the living God has great love for the future of his people and will do the most miraculous things to ensure that future. This includes giving people unexpected and perhaps supernatural favor with each other. It is a great example for anyone who believes his story has already ended.

I see an important lesson embedded in the Book of Ruth. When I have read these passages in the Bible in the past, I always marveled at how wonderful Ruth was. Certainly she was a very special person. It is remarkable, however, that two women who should have been enemies loved each other so much! It is obvious that God's hand was at work in their lives.

I came to believe the exceptional favor God gave Ruth and Naomi is available to us in our relationships. God is today the same as He was yesterday, and He still works miracles in the lives of His hurting people. I experienced God's favor personally with the healing of my relationship with my mother-in-law and with my sister (Chapters 7 and 8). God's grace was released in those relationships when prayer became an important part of our time together.

The story of Ruth speaks to me about how the grace of God works in relationships. Some of us have family members, casual friends, or associates at work to whom we just can't seem to relate. We believe it will always be this way. We are convinced when it comes to these particular relationships, it is a dead-end street. I wonder what would happen if we prayed for God to give us the kind of favor that Ruth and Naomi had with each other. What if we prayed for Him to give us great love and devotion for those people and pierce our conscience about what we say when we speak to them? What if we prayed for their thoughts and attitudes, as well as our own, to be brought into captivity to the will of the living God?

Could our Heavenly Father give us the same kind of grace at our dead-end-street that He gave Ruth and Naomi? Relationships are two-way streets and one can only take responsibility for his own attitude. However, what if God's grace was sought for healing? Could we allow the living God to show off His expertise in making the improbable happen? What might the outcome be for His kingdom's work? How might our lives unfold differently?

We know the story of Naomi as it is recorded in the Book of Ruth, but is it possible that we *also* have stories that are waiting to be written and shared with future generations of believers? Every day our life narrative is being recorded. Pursue God's grace and pray about your troubled relationships that seem to be on a dead-end street! Wait for God to do the improbable, and bless your entire family line by your faithfulness!

Matthew 14:28-30

Then Peter called to him, "LORD, if it's really you, tell me to come to you by walking on water."

"All right, come," Jesus said. So Peter went over the side of the boat and walked on the water toward Jesus. But when he looked around at the high waves, he was terrified and began to sink...

CHAPTER EIGHTEEN

It's Only a Pair of Shoes

Victorious Living Depends on Finding God's Priorities

$\mathcal{I}$ stood at the sink with one of my favorite pair of shoes in my hands trying to carefully remove the mud that had coated them on an unexpected trip outside. I was in the church kitchen where I had earlier placed a few trays of food in the refrigerator for our Bible study that night. While I was in the fellowship hall setting up the tables with handouts and other materials, some diligent soul decided to lock the kitchen for the evening. I did not have a key for any of the three front doors of the kitchen that opened into the fellowship hall. A frantic phone call to the person in charge of facilities provided the information that the key I used for the front door of the church would also work on the one outside door of the kitchen. The problem was that I had to go outside to unlock this door, and the area where I needed to walk was still wet and muddy from the surprise March snowstorm we had a few days before. To get to that outside door, I had to go all the way around to the other side of the building. There was no avoiding the mud no matter where I stepped!

When I put on my good pair of loafers earlier in the day, I did not entertain the idea that I might end the evening walking in mud. I was standing at the sink fretting out loud about my situation when Mary, one of the table leaders for the study, joined me. Mary has always been one of my favorite people, and her witness for the Lord has had a huge impact on my life in a wonderful, compelling way. Without saying a word, Mary took one of the shoes out of my hand and with a paper towel started to wipe away some of the mud. She stood there quietly working until the shoe was clean. Immediately, the Holy Spirit was speaking to me reminding me that I was letting a pair of shoes distract me from what was really important that evening. Thirty or more ladies were about to join me in prayer and study of God's Word, and my focus was on a pair of muddy shoes! The real treasure of my day was about to be forfeited because I lost my focus on what the Lord had set before me.

When I was younger, my favorite uncle modeled the importance of paying attention to the heartfelt priorities of one's life. He did a wonderful job of reframing expectations to meet the needs of the person he was helping. I will never forget when almost fifty years ago, Uncle Babe attempted to teach me how to drive. This same uncle was the one who taught me to ride a bike when I was eight years old. Others tried without much success, but he had a way about him that instilled confidence when I tried new things. I will never forget the empowerment I experienced when he let go of my bicycle, and I rode triumphantly down the road.

I had many traumatic experiences when I first tried to learn to drive a car, especially one with a manual gear shift. I still remember my frantic father yelling at me about engaging the clutch as we rolled down several hills. The final outing with my father ended with him screaming at me for making a sudden turn on the highway near our home. Somewhere in the middle of that situation was a truck bearing down on us! My father just couldn't take any more of that kind of stress, and his exasperation over my struggles totally drained from my spirit any confidence I might have had. Ironically, my father was a teacher at my high school, and troublesome, high-spirited students came his way every day. However, the difficulties of dealing with troublemakers at school could not compare to the anxiety of trying to teach a teenage daughter to drive.

I was taking a driver's education class at school but found my driving time very limited. It usually took place in secure locations such as the school's parking lot. It seemed that my teacher wanted to extend his life expectancy past the end of my class!

It looked as if I were never going to learn to drive. I was beginning to get accustomed to the idea that I would have to accept failure and be forever dependent on public transportation. My uncle Babe, however, was not about to let the same niece who learned to ride a bicycle with his guidance fail to learn how to drive a car. He had a car with an automatic transmission, and one night on a deserted country road, he turned the driving over to me. I tried to talk him out of letting me take the wheel, but my stubborn uncle refused to let me say no. So here we were driving on a road where no one else who would be at risk with me as the driver. I started to feel pretty good because I was sitting behind the steering wheel and covering ground without anyone yelling at me or getting hysterical. At one point in our evening experience, I asked my uncle, "How am I doing?" My uncle responded calmly saying, "You are doing really great. Now if you could drive on the right side of the road instead of the left, you would be perfect!"

This story was repeated over and over in my family throughout the years. A year before my Uncle Babe died, he told the story one last time at the local funeral home during the visitation time for his beloved wife, my Aunt Bette. My uncle had been the "youngest" eighty-year-old man one would ever meet, but then he suffered a stroke that affected his cognitive abilities. He also developed violent tendencies when he became agitated, and that necessitated his being placed in a nursing home. My Aunt Bette could not allow him to be there alone, so she also moved to the nursing home to help him secure some happiness in this lonely place.

I stood next to Uncle Babe during the long visitation period and frequently offered my hands to him and told him, "My hands are freezing cold; could you please warm them up?" The touching of our hands seemed to spark something in him. Many times I could not understand what he was saying to me, but suddenly he became very lucid as he told the story of my driving on the wrong side of the road one more time. His eyes lit up as he remembered teaching me to drive and patiently telling me to drive on the right side of the road.

I have cherished my experiences with my uncle all these years and marveled at how he could zero in on what was important and let the rest blur into the background. Had he not taught me that, I would have missed gaining the confidence I needed to accomplish many things in my life that frightened me.

Recently my adult daughter, Jennifer, delighted me with her story about Uncle Babe. I had no idea that he also helped her learn to drive. When she was sixteen years old, my uncle and aunt visited us, and he took her out for a driving lesson on the outer loop of our city. She also was just learning to drive when he surprised her and placed her behind the wheel of his car. As cars sped past her, she drove at thirty to thirty-five miles per hour, and he kept telling her to ignore the other drivers and not to worry about them. My uncle simply focused on what he thought was important. He didn't worry about anything else.

My daughter has had confidence in herself all her life and has been successful in teaching, singing, ballet, running a small business, and many other things. She does a wonderful job of witnessing for the Lord. I know the confidence my uncle helped her achieve is giving her the motivation to strive for what is important in life.

Getting my shoes muddy at the church and having Mary

help clean them reminded me again of the lesson my uncle taught my daughter and me: Focus on what is the greatest priority and forget about everything else that is happening. The strange thing about that experience is that the Lord gave me yet another opportunity to learn this same lesson with another pair of muddy shoes. He knew that He was dealing with a slow learner.

My husband and I have friends who are going through a rough patch in their lives. Larry has played golf with his friend for over twenty-five years, and I have known his wife for almost as long. Our hearts have ached for our friend as we have witnessed his profound suffering with cancer over the past three years. We have looked for ways to share our faith with our friends, and continually we balance a need to do that with a desire not to intrude and create discomfort for them. Expressing one's faith is such a personal thing.

We prayed with our friend for the first time a year and a half after his second bout with this horrible disease. After undergoing painful and debilitating radiation and chemotherapy, he then had surgery, and we asked if we could pray for him. We felt the Lord's presence in that hospital room, but since that time we recognized no other opportunities to do anything except relate that we and others were praying for him to have a complete recovery.

After not seeing our friend for several weeks, we learned that he was headed to a cancer hospital in another state for another operation. We made plans to meet him and his wife at their home and go to dinner before they left. The day we were to meet them, I began to feel an urging from the Holy Spirit that Larry and I must pray with them that evening in their home. The Holy Spirit was focusing my spirit on my friends' greatest need and His kingdom's work, but I wasn't confident the evening would provide a comfort level for the four of us to pray together. I called a wonderful Christian friend and asked her to pray with me that the Lord would provide an opportunity for us to pray and also give us His words for our prayer.

After a delightful dinner, the four of us went to see a house that was being built in our friends' neighborhood. We were told that it was owned by a local celebrity and was the largest one ever built in the neighborhood. Nothing can stop two women from finding and seeing a house like that, and the two men good-naturedly followed along. By the time we found the house, it was almost dark. We didn't notice that as we walked around the grounds, we were absolutely caking our shoes with Georgia red clay mud!

When we returned home, the four of us laughed and plotted how we were going to clean our shoes. My friend Betty was horrified to see my beautiful flats coated with mud. She looked at me and said, "If we can't return your shoes to their original condition, we will have to travel to the shoe store in the mountains where you purchased them and buy another pair." (That would have not been a sacrifice for two ladies who love to shop!)

I laughed and told her, "They are just a pair of shoes." I remembered what was important.

A few minutes later, the four of us joined hands and prayed about Bob's impending surgery. We even asked the Lord to heal our friend and not let him experience any debilitation that would cause him not to be able to play golf again. (There was fear that the surgery would result in the loss of use of his right arm.) As of this writing, our friend has resumed playing golf and has maintained nearly normal function of his arm. We continue to wait and see what the Lord's plan is for his life. I can see that the Holy Spirit used muddy shoes that evening to knit our spirits together, so we could join together in prayer. We were able to focus on what was important and let the muddy shoes blur into the background.

My Uncle Babe could not have possibly known the monumental importance of the lessons he taught me in the days I spent with him. It is only by the Lord's hand that the last few lucid minutes I had with my uncle were spent with him talking about me driving on the wrong side of the road and his encouraging words.

I remember in Scripture (Matthew 14: 28-30) when Jesus summoned Peter to join Him as He walked on the water outside their boat. Everything was going well until Peter looked around and became distracted by the high waves. Peter was terrified and began to sink, for he lost sight of what was important as he walked beside the Lord on the water.

How many occasions have there been in our lives when the Lord was waiting to do something monumental for His kingdom's work, but we let the world's distractions get in the way? How many faith opportunities have we bypassed and sank back into the world's view of what is important? I don't want to forget the gift my uncle left in my spirit.

Pray for spiritual eyesight so that you can look at "muddy shoe" situations in your life and focus on what is important as you see God's hand at work. Strive to walk on the water in faith as you walk along with the Lord Jesus and not let the distractions of the world cause you to sink!

2 Samuel 6:14-15

And David danced before the LORD with all his might, wearing a priestly tunic. So, David and all Israel brought up the Ark of the Lord with much shouting and blowing of trumpets.

Psalm 30:11

You have turned my mourning into joyful dancing. You have taken away my clothes of mourning and clothed me with joy!

Psalm 149:3

Praise his name with dancing, accompanied by tambourine and harp.

CHAPTER NINETEEN

Senior Prom

Don't Sit on the Sidelines of Life—Dance

*H*ere I was at the age of sixty-four attending my first senior prom! The young students in our church, who called themselves "Mission Possible Kids," were holding a senior prom for all the senior citizens in our church. They staged the complete event with flowers, refreshments, and music mainly from the 1940's. Even though I was just a child in the 1940's, I have always loved the music from that era. The parade of pictures that flashed on the giant screen in our fellowship hall made me feel like I was back in that period of time.

My high school senior class of 1962 did not have a prom. Instead, we had a senior trip to Washington D.C. My trip to the nation's capital was memorable and worth every moment I contributed to the fundraising efforts to finance the trip. Even though I usually disliked selling anything, I was the top earner of magazine subscriptions for our class. I wanted our senior class to make that trip. However, in later years I wished that somehow our class could have had both a prom and the trip.

There are many advantages to having a senior prom at my age! I was able to have my husband of forty-three years as my date, so I didn't have to look for some unsuspecting young man to escort me. Also, even though I am not much of a dancer, I did not have to sit on the sidelines watching everyone else dance. Expectations are so different when you have reached your sixties. Freedom arrives as inhibitions depart!

My nine-year-old granddaughter Alyssa and my eleven-year-old grandson Brandon happily and joyfully asked me to dance. Alyssa said, "I had a really good time when we were dancing!" She surely could not have enjoyed it as much as I did.

Brandon said, "We really rocked the place!" I am sure if I had attended a senior prom in 1962, I would not have heard those encouraging words from my date.

Meaningful conversation was always a problem with my dates in 1962 because I was very shy. It was not a problem at the senior prom at my church because many of the youngsters were eager to engage us seniors in conversation about the good old days. My husband and I loved telling them about the cost of things and the games we played when we were growing up. The strange thing about those memories was that they didn't seem that long ago to us.

Pictures were taken by one of the adults attending the dance who later gave them out to all the participants. I am sure that years from now when my grandchildren are grown, they will have a good time sharing those pictures with their children and telling them about attending their grandmother's senior prom. The best part was all the caring hearts that worked together to create joy for the seniors at our church. Joy should always be in our spirits when we are welcoming the Lord into our midst. I am sure that the Lord Himself attended our dance.

Sometimes I have an urge to dance with joy just as King

David did when the ark was being returned to Israel after the enemy had taken it many months earlier. So many times I just sit on my hands when joy is beckoning to me.

I now welcome opportunities to dance with King David's exuberance with loved ones. I am sure that King David would have liked the dancing at our prom because the children and adults dancing together had elation written all over their faces. Psalm 30:11 proclaims, "You have turned my mourning into joyful dancing. You have taken away my clothes of mourning and clothed me with joy!" Many of us at this "senior prom" were clothed with joy.

I am also sure there were angels surrounding all the young people as they worked so hard to bring pleasure to the guests. Sometimes I recognize the presence of angels when I feel a fresh breeze sweep through my spirit, and a quiet, peaceful feeling comes over me. I am certain that the living God smiled as He saw the dancing, laughing, and loving that took place in His fellowship hall.

A few years ago our pastor played a CD of the song "I Hope You Dance"[7] during our church service. The lyrics rang out in the sanctuary beckoning us not to lose our sense of wonder about life and to never take life for granted. The song encouraged us to notice the majesty of the ocean and all the other breathtaking moments that have been created for us in nature, and to give faith a chance in our lives. The message of the song was that when we have the choice in our lives to participate or just watch the world go by, we should not sit on the sidelines-we should dance!

I don't want to ever lose an opportunity to dance and grasp the moments that beckon to me throughout my life. Some of these God-given moments come to me through the wonder in my grandchildren's eyes and through the imagination of other children who cross my path. They come through family members as they fill my life with meaning, through my pastors' devotion and vision for the church, and through the reflection of Christ-filled lives that surround me.

Some day when we leave this earth, we will dance with loved ones who have already gone ahead of us. We will sit with the Lord and listen to music as all beings in heaven dance with praise and joy!

BARBARA J. CORNELIUS

Isaiah 64:4

For since the world began, no ear has heard, and no eye has seen a God like you, who works for those who wait for him!

CHAPTER TWENTY

Lessons Learned from Bubbles

When Situations Are Darkest God Steps In

$\mathscr{I}$ watched my three-year-old granddaughters, Jacie and Abigail, as they surrounded themselves with bubbles on my front porch. They were giggling as they tried to catch some of the bubbles and transport them across the porch. They watched to see how far past the steps and into the sky their bubbles traveled. They even identified some of the bubbles as baby, mommy, and daddy bubbles. Their joy and imagination increased with each dipping of their wands into the bubble mixture.

As I watched these joy-filled little girls, I remembered all the times I had done bubble activities with my students. I taught elementary and middle school science for over thirty years before I retired a few years ago. I conducted bubble labs, bubble workshops for fellow teachers, and even placed individual students in

143

giant bubbles! Everyone likes to blow bubbles. Somewhere in one's spirit, light seems to spring forth while blowing bubbles and watching them float away.

When I did bubble labs with my middle-school students, I would have them place some bubble mixture on the table where they sat and use a straw to blow a bubble. They would observe the color changes of the bubble before it burst. At first they would see the colors of the rainbow as the bubble refracted light, but just before the bubble burst, it would turn to a blackish color.

Being enclosed in a bubble can be a fantastic experience. I accomplished this by placing students in a plastic pool of bubble solution and then lowering a giant wand around them. When the wand was lifted, a giant bubble surrounded them. I once enclosed the principal of an elementary school I was visiting in a huge bubble. He remarked, "This is so cool!" I can still see this six-foot man smiling as the bubble surrounded him.

However, as I watched my granddaughters delight in the experience of blowing hundreds of bubbles, I pondered the analogy of a bubble turning black before it bursts and life experiences that enclose us in painful ways before the situation suddenly changes. Many times in life we feel trapped by conditions that seem to be hopeless, and when we see no happy solution ahead of us, despair sets in. Human eyes simply do not see what God sees, and human intelligence cannot perceive what God perceives.

When the Israelites were perched on the edge of Egypt trying to make their grand exit with Moses leading the way, they had the Red Sea ahead of them, mountains on both sides, and 600 chariots with Egyptian warriors charging at them from behind. They felt completely enclosed in a hopeless situation and promptly expressed to Moses their feelings about their plight. Just when everything was at its darkest, the living God parted the Red Sea, allowing the Israelites to cross and then closing the sea behind them and destroying their enemies.

How many times have we been in an experience when, just after our darkest hour, the living God miraculously interceded to give us a glorious solution? Sometimes, it is much later when we see that the "bubble" has burst, and we then realize that we had been set free days, weeks, or even years earlier. I once was in a painful situation in my profession, and my self-esteem took a direct hit from the way I was being treated. I gave much thought to leaving my job, and when I shared my predicament with a Christian friend, she asked me, "Why don't you just quit?"

I pondered her question, and replied to her, "The Lord has not released me to leave!" I knew in my heart I would have peace about quitting if that was His will. I remained in that position for three years, and at the end of that time I experienced relief. I knew that the Lord rewarded me with a gift for waiting on Him. I had a new humility in my spirit, which was not debilitating low self-esteem, but a glimmer of what was in His Spirit when He put all His majesty aside to come to this Earth as a replacement for us. He came with great humility in order to be our substitute.

I once shared this story with a friend whom I had not seen for many years. He lived in the home town I had left over forty years previously. He shared with me one of the darkest times in his career, when he was falsely accused of embezzling funds from the school system where he worked. He saw his entire career and reputation being destroyed, and he kept praying for the Lord to intercede and make things right for him. His burdens just seemed to increase! He had the financial burden of hiring a lawyer, loss of sleep, and days filled with anxiety. Still, he remained faithful to the Lord and sought Him at the altar of his church each Sunday. Suddenly, when this situation seemed to be the most dismal, it changed completely. The person who had stolen the money confessed to the authorities, and my friend was completely exonerated.

My friend waited on the Lord, and He rewarded his faithfulness. He told me, "I received a gift that I would never have sought, but I gratefully accept it. There was nothing I would take in exchange for the gift of watching the living God act on my behalf."

The two years before my daughter met her second husband were a very stressful period in her life. She was single with two young children for four years. She wondered if God planned for her to be single for the rest of her life and if He would give her the strength to wait on Him to determine His will for her life. I gave her the prophecy the Lord gave to me, "You will be married in two years, and you should claim Isaiah 64:4 as you wait."

This scripture, "Since the world began, no ear has heard, and no eye has seen a God like You, Who works for those who wait for Him!" gave her much strength. Two years later, my daughter and her about-to-be new husband carried crosses with this scripture as they spoke their wedding vows.

It is never easy to stand and wait for the Lord when we are mired in a stressful situation. It is so difficult to trust God when we cannot see what lies ahead. This is what faith is all about. He will act on our behalf in His timing.

Someone once described the "divine domino effect" that is in place when we put our prayers in the throne room of the living God. God will act in His wisdom, grace, and power until each "domino" has moved the next "domino" in our situation to give a complete answer and His full will is done.

Even when we are in our darkest moments and our minds tell us not to believe, the miracle of what our God can do is a reality, not of the world, but of the heavens. Sometimes God is telling us to wait on Him because His solution is really going to be amazing, and we will like it when we see it! Wait until each "divine domino" has fallen and trust the living God with the prayers you leave in His throne room.

Proverbs 31:10, 25-26, 28

Who can find a virtuous and capable wife? She is clothed with strength and dignity, and she laughs with no fear of the future. When she speaks, her words are wise, and kindness is the rule when she gives instructions. Her children stand and bless her.

Psalm 147:3

He heals the brokenhearted, binding up their wounds.

Nehemiah 8:10

The joy of the LORD is your strength!

Exodus 20:6

But I lavish my love on those who love me and obey my commands, even for a thousand generations.

CHAPTER TWENTY ONE

She Walks in Courage

When Tragedies Strike, Follow God's Footprints

$\mathscr{I}$ looked at Mother as she stood in the fellowship hall of our church waiting for her ninetieth birthday party to begin. She had never looked lovelier in her white pants suit and shimmering silver jacket. Tables with delicious food and beautiful roses were waiting for the seventy invited guests. Several out-of-town relatives had driven many hours so they could surprise her and be among the guests. We had planned a wonderful program of music to be presented by my husband, daughter, and grandchildren, and I prepared a short speech to honor her on this special day.

Shortly before the party was to begin, we looked out the window, and to our amazement, the rain on this March 1st day had turned into large flakes of snow! Snow, which is rare in Athens, Georgia, began to accumulate and change the outdoor

149

scene into a winter wonderland. I prayed for the Lord to make mother's ninetieth birthday party a memorable one, and He had answered that prayer in a surprising way. Our large celebration turned into an intimate gathering, and our prepared program had to be condensed into a few songs. Our pastor came and told us we needed to hurry home as quickly as possible because the roads were becoming treacherous.

All during the following week, we fed our friends with leftover food, and I felt like I was beginning a new career as a caterer. The roses became centerpieces at a Bible study two days later and then went home with some of the ladies in attendance. What was my mother's response to her birthday party? Mother, who never gave up her joy without a struggle, said that she felt as if she had been treated like a queen! Her comment meant to me that her weather-shortened party was a total success!

Many times in the months since Mother's party, I have shared all the ways the Lord blessed us on that day (including the safety we experienced during several frightening moments on the hour and a half trip home which is an usual fifteen minute drive). I spent months planning Mother's party to make certain I attended to every detail, and her attitude about that day kept me from feeling much disappointment.

It is my mother's positive outlook on life and great faith that has nourished her family's faith all our lives. When her nine-year-old son died (Chapter 3 and Chapter 6), she was a young woman in her thirties. The doctor had told her that Bobby had only about three months to live. Mother had chosen not to believe the doctor because she could not accept the thought of losing her only son to a disease that had not even been diagnosed.

After Bobby's funeral, my mother did not want any of the flowers brought to our house. When my cousin and I took some of the bows that were on the flowers to our home, she wept at the sight of them. She worked the night shift at the local hospital for the next four years to help her make it through the nights without her son. During the day she found sleep in her exhaustion.

Mother could have framed the rest of her life with this tragedy. However, even though her suffering was profound, she found courage for living that could only come from her faith and trust in the living God. She later said, "I had two young daughters who needed me, and I could not succumb to my grief. I had to go on living for them." Somehow, she found the inner strength to continue her life with her family who desperately needed her in order to have hope for the future.

I am sure that Mother did not walk alone on the paths that led her from great sorrow to victorious living. She was a registered nurse for over forty years and worked in obstetrics for most of that time. Once she was walking toward a young father carrying his new baby in her arms, and she slipped and fell on the newly-waxed floor. She did not drop the baby but instead landed on the floor with the baby nestled safely in her arms. The father had tears in his eyes when she handed the baby to him. I am positive there were angels present that day to protect the baby and Mother from another tragedy. Perhaps it was no coincidence that Mother had a ministry in making angel food cakes for her friends' birthdays!

Mother has always had a heart for the needs of children and for anyone who was experiencing physical suffering. I remember one occasion a few years after my brother's death when Mother spent the night with a friend dying of cancer. She went to work the next morning without any sleep. During the last three years of my brother's life, she and my father had very few good nights of sleep. They would lie awake listening for his call to them. Now she was pouring out herself as a living sacrifice for someone else who needed her. This kind of courage for living comes from a divine source- the living God.

I know that my spiritual life was influenced by my mother's courage and faith. One of the most nourishing ingredients for faith is pure, unadulterated joy. Mother, in her long life, has never forfeited her joy for very long periods of time. I believe that is because joy has nothing to do with one's circumstances. Joy can be present in all situations because it comes from having a close, intimate relationship with the Lord. Nehemiah 8:10 says, "The joy of the Lord is your strength!"

One source of enjoyment for Mother has always been traveling to new places. In the forty years that she and my father were married they took a trip to a destination several hours or a few days away, every summer when she had vacation time. They traveled to most states in our country. After my father's death Mother worked one more year before she retired and then began traveling out of the country for the first time. She visited Egypt, Greece, England, Italy, Scotland, and Israel. My favorite picture of Mother was taken in Egypt, where she is perched high on a camel. I don't know how many angels the Lord sent that day to keep her safe on that beast, but more than a few family members have grinned upon seeing that picture. I know God smiled when the picture was taken.

I believe one of the greatest miracles that the Lord gives us is letting us see that the end of the story does not come with our death or the death of someone we love. He breathes courage and faith into our countenance after we have said farewell to a beloved person. He has done that for my mother. Our God knows what it is like to lose an only Son and His glory and power are revealed in and through us as we endure such a loss.

Hymns like "It Is Well with My Soul," "What a Friend We Have in Jesus," and countless others were written by people after they had suffered horrible tragedies in their lives. The living God breathed inspiration into their spirits as they reached to Him for comfort. Thousands and thousands of people have experienced the comfort of the Holy Spirit as they have sung these songs. Mother told me recently that she wakes up frequently singing a hymn that just seems to come to her during the night.

After the death of my brother, I saw my mother pour out her life into her family, friends, and others, like a living offering to the Lord. She has never wavered in her faith. I believe that, in selflessly serving others, she has brought joy to our Heavenly Father because He could see that her witness brought honor and glory to Him. Her life has mattered not only to herself and her family, but also to the kingdom.

I have a painting in my home that was done by my maternal grandmother. This was the grandmother who taught a Sunday school class of seventy-five to one hundred people (Chapter 15). She gave me the painting several years before she died, and it was many years before I realized what I had. The painting, which is now in the prayer room of my house, shows Abraham leading Isaac to be sacrificed. The faith that Abraham demonstrated in his willingness to give up his son on that fateful day has blessed all of the Lord's people every day since. Exodus 20:6 tells us that the living God blesses those that love Him for a thousand generations.

My mother's faith and steadfastness will enrich the lives of many generations. She walks in courage and she walks with the Lord. Let all of her children, grandchildren, and great grandchildren stand and bless her.

Each individual person's life is important not just for himself or herself personally. His or her life matters for everyone in their domain, for the kingdom's work, and for the glory and honor of the living God. A person who walks in footprints of courage and faith may send God's light through a thousand generations! What a precious gift we have been given by our Lord that we could matter that much to the world and to His kingdom.

Psalm 16:11

You will show me the way of life, granting me the joy of your presence, and the pleasures of living with you forever.

Philippians 3:20-21

But we are all citizens of heaven, where the LORD Jesus lives. And we are eagerly waiting for Him to return as our Savior! He will take these weak mortal bodies of ours and change them into glorious bodies like his own, using the same power with which he will bring everything, under his control.

Revelation 21:4

"He will wipe away every tear from their eyes, and there will be no more death or sorrow or crying or pain. All these things are gone forever."

CHAPTER TWENTY TWO

Where Was the Miracle?

Faithful Lives Have Glorious Endings

*W*e stood in the parking lot sobbing in each other's arms. My son and I prayed so fervently for Carla to be healed and for her to be able to continue her blessed life with her husband and family on this earth. She had such a beautiful singing voice and was a wonderful witness for the Lord! She loved children and so wanted to be a mother, either by giving birth or by adoption. She had struggled valiantly with a diseased liver for three years and was in desperate need of a liver transplant. For reasons that only God Himself can explain, the liver was only a few hours away when she slipped into eternity.

Where was the miracle her family and all of us who loved her asked the living God to give us? God sits on His throne and sees our most crucial needs and our desperation to keep our loved ones with us, especially when they are young and their lives are just beginning. He has our hopes and dreams in His hands, and He knows that our suffering and pain is like a cloudy mist over our lives. Surely He loves us and wants to protect us from personal devastation. Where was our miracle?

My introduction to death came at a very early age when my brother, Bobby, died (Chapters 3, 6, and 21). From the time Bobby was a year old until he passed away, he ran a fever every day. The doctors could not decide what was slowly taking life from his body. They spoke to my parents about exploratory surgery months before he died. When my mother told Bobby about the impending surgery, he said, "They're too late." How it is possible that a child so young can sense that death is coming soon?

My parents sent me to the next door neighbor's house the night Bobby died. Even though it has been over fifty years, I can still hear my aunt coming to the door to tell our neighbor the news. The devastation of that announcement stayed with me for much of my life as I suffered through depression and torment over the thought that the wrong child had died. How could God let that happen? My sick brother took on the qualities of a saintly child in my mind. I remember all the people who came to the house with meals, love, and prayers. I remember the pastors who came to pray for the healing of the special little boy. Where was the miracle?

Throughout my life the Lord has consistently given me proof of His loving presence and has even given me experiences that have made me feel as if a door of heaven has been opened to me.

Almost twenty years ago, I sat in a church sanctuary on Christmas Eve and had a glimpse of what awaits us in heaven. The candlelight service being conducted was beautiful and joy was overflowing in the hearts of the congregation. Our choir director was sitting on a stool at the front, and even though she was in the final days of her long fight with cancer, she was singing with happiness. Her portable oxygen tank at her feet faded into the background as her voice filled that moment in time.

I looked at her and I saw a person who could not possibly be sick. She looked healthy and better than I had seen her look for several years. Her face was glowing as if she was already in heaven, and it was if she had been given a new body. I could hear the Holy Spirit revealing to me that I was getting a glimpse of heaven. This precious young woman in her thirties died two weeks later.

Another remarkable experience came a few years later after my husband's father passed away. I had a very unusual and vivid dream. Our family had worried so much about my father-in-law's lack of profession of faith. He was a very challenging individual with habits that caused much grief for his family. He refused any invitations to attend church, and certainly, even in the days when his health was rapidly failing, would not let a pastor come and speak to him. Strangely though, many Sundays would find him listening to pastors' sermons on television. When he died, the family felt heartache because they didn't believe he had ever been saved.

Two years after his passing, I had the only dream I have ever had about him. He was sitting far away from me on the green grass of a river bank with his legs crossed. I knew him instantly because he always liked to sit that way in a chair in his home. As I approached him and saw his smiling face, I was amazed that he looked so young and healthy. There was no missing the radiance that surrounded his whole body and the feeling of great love that radiated from him. Even though I was totally convinced it was my father-in-law, I had never seen him look that wonderful when he was alive. As I approached him, he got up and started walking with me along the river bank. I knew then we were in heaven, and he was greeting me. Later, my husband told me how much his father loved the river and that would have been where he was happiest.

Later, a close friend shared with me the dream of heaven her ailing father had two months before he died. Even though it was seven years since his death, she had vivid memories of what he had told her. As she revealed the details of her father's dream, I felt a wave of excitement sweep over me. There were so many similarities between the two dreams! I felt that I was receiving confirmation that what I saw was a real glimpse of heaven. I told her I was in the same place in my dream.

A few years ago, I had the opportunity to visualize the reunion that awaits all believers when they reach heaven. I traveled with my husband from our home in Georgia to attend a three-day Christian women's retreat in Indiana. Larry was going to stay with family members while I attended the retreat. He was excited about my going because he had attended the men's retreat a few months previously and knew it would be a wonderful experience that we would be able to share.

On the last night of the retreat, I walked with the other women along the long path to the chapel for a life-changing event that I will never forget! The path was lighted with candles and friends and family members were singing to us as we walked by. I knew not to look for any family members from Georgia because I was too far from home.

As I walked into the candlelit chapel and got close to the front, I was shocked to see my daughter and two grandchildren from Georgia standing with my husband's family. My three-year-old granddaughter reached for me. I tearfully took her into my arms and touched the arms of my daughter and five-year-old grandson for a few moments before finishing my walk to the altar. My husband had dropped me off at the retreat and immediately turned around and traveled eleven hundred miles round trip to get my daughter and grandchildren, so they could surprise me and be in that chapel for a few minutes with me!

My heart was absolutely flooded with the greatest joy that I can ever remember as I looked at each family member. I immediately had a vision of the reunion that awaits me in heaven! I remember looking at each family member standing there with happiness and love written all over their faces. I especially remember my mother-in-law, who has since passed away, and seeing her face as she stood in the pew. Elation with what we all were experiencing shone on her countenance. I am looking forward to seeing her and all other family members in heaven and participating in the most joyous reunion that will ever be!

Through the years as tragedies have unfolded before me, I have pondered the miracles that continue to happen as I see the living God in everything around me. I have seen too many miracles, especially in the last ten years, not to trust Him with my life. I know that the greatest miracle that ever happened occurred when Jesus rose from the tomb to conquer death. Death happens not only to our bodies, but in our souls when we carry our brokenness and refuse to give it up. I was reborn and made new in my spirit when I accepted God's grace of forgiveness. I am filled with great anticipation of shedding this earthly body and becoming completely new and healed in body and spirit.

I have read several books written by people who had visions, dreams, and out of body experiences after they were declared dead and then came back to life. Many of them validate what I have felt in my own spirit. I know heaven must be a beautiful, breathtaking, and exhilarating place. Our Heavenly Father could not have created anything less for us than to be in His presence for eternity.

Some would say that heaven is a quiet and uneventful place because all the souls there have finished their work on earth. I disagree. I believe that heaven has something like a spiritual "mission control center" that focuses on the work to be completed to reach all the lost before Jesus returns to Earth. The Book of Revelation discloses the greatest drama that will ever unfold in the end times as Jesus claims His victory over Satan and his army of darkness. From now until that time, our Heavenly Father is continually looking for people who will do His kingdom's work and evangelize with hearts on fire for Him. As the number of days diminishes until that final battle, I believe that the intensity of preparation in heaven heightens.

A friend whose wife died of cancer told of his prayers for his wife to be healed. He said that one day, while he was praying, he heard the Lord's voice as clearly as he had ever heard any human voice. He heard God tell him, "I need your wife in heaven."

Why would God call loved ones to heaven when we desperately need them with us on earth? How is it that He needs them more? Somehow, in a way we cannot comprehend, His glory must be at stake. I know that can be the only answer because when we hurt and grieve, He hurts and grieves with us. I love the idea that when I reach heaven, God will have work for me to do that will bring pleasure to Him and joy to my spirit. I so want to glorify the living God!

In my spirit I see in heaven my young friend Carla who died at the age of thirty-three. Her face is glowing as her stunning voice fills the heavenlies. I can see her surrounded by angels as she rocks little babies in her lap and sings God's praises. I can see her as she energetically gives her input to those engaged in planning the kingdom's work for when Jesus again returns to Earth in all His glory. She is all that God meant for her to be in heaven. Many, many more souls will join her to declare victory in Jesus when the last day of history has been written.

Our loved ones who knew the Lord when they left this earth are now residing in the miracle of God's grace and glory. The future holds for us a wonderful reunion with them! Tears of joy will dampen our faces when we see them. Our exhilaration will be felt all throughout heaven! Praise the living God for who He is! Praise Him! Praise Him!

ANSWERED PRAYER
by Barbara Cornelius

I prayed and asked my Heavenly Father:

To let me know His character and His ways,
And He placed me with others who had a contagious hunger for this
same desire.

To send someone to guide and comfort the son of my blood,
And He sent a prophet from Ghana who became the son of my
heart.

To allow me to see Him in His majestic glory,
And He revealed His awesomeness in His daily masterpieces in the
sky.

To give me a pure heart so that I could see Him,
And He sent friends to come and pray with me as a loved one lay
dying.

To see a loved one healed as death became a close companion,
And He brought a miracle through the hands of doctors who knew
His voice.

To soothe friends suffering from despair of loss and pain from this
world,

And He laid my hands upon their shoulders, touching them through
my body.

To send comfort and hope for my young friend who was waiting for
a new kidney,
And He sent a pastor who had traveled this road ahead of her with
courage and faith.

To give me spiritual eyes so that I could see one of His heavenly
angels of light,
And He sent me friends surrounded by light who were full of His
strength and joy!

Note from the author: Have you ever wished to speak directly to God? Have you ever wished He had a cell phone? Well He does!—Jeremiah 33:3 "Call to Me and I will answer you and tell you great and unsearchable things you do not know."

Photo Gallery

My father, Harold Spencer
(Millionaire Teacher)

My Uncle, Francis "Babe"
Spencer
(It's Only a Pair of Shoes)

My brother Bobby and Me
(God's Lost and Found Department)

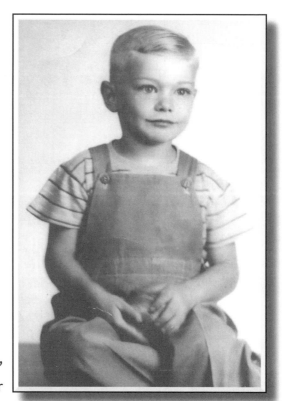

Robert "Bobby"
Dale Spencer

Grandson Brandon Wyatt
(Young Prayer Warrior)

Granddaughter Alyssa Wyatt
(Red Silk Dress)

Cornelius Grandchildren (L to R): Brandon Wyatt,
Benjamin Snipes, Alyssa Wyatt holding Robert Cornelius,
Abigail Cornelius, Jacie Snipes, Jeffrey Cornelius

165

Granddaughter Alyssa in a bubble at
her 4th birthday party

My Grandson
Brandon and
son Jeff blowing
bubbles after
Jeff and Julie's
wedding

Granddaughters Jacie Snipes and Abigail Cornelius
(Lessons Learned From Bubbles)

My daughter
Jennifer Snipes and
her husband Earl
(Daughter
Reclaimed)

My mother, Martha Spencer
(Walking in Courage)

My mother enjoying a camel ride!

Our friends from Ghana—Joseph, Karen, "little
Joseph" Essiful-Ansah (Jamie's Story/Daughter
Reclaimed/Promised Son)

My son Jeff and daughter-in-law Julie on
their wedding day

My Sister, Sue Hannah, and Me
(Sisters Rejoined)

My Mother-in-Law Vera
Cornelius
(Hearts Rejoined)

My Beloved Husband, Larry Cornelius,
Singing at a Recent Performance
(The Gift)

Endnotes

1 **Chapter One, Jamie's Story**
Clinging Cross, handmade by Jane Davis, Copyright 2003

2 **Chapter Two, Defying the Laws of Physics**
Billy Graham, Angels: God's Secret Agents. New York: Doubleday & Co. Inc. 1975

3 **Chapter Five, Flight of the Bumblebee**
Barbara Cornelius and Jolaine Whitehead, Take Out Science and Math to Digest at Home, © 2000, Barrow County School System

4 **Chapter Six, Grace Not Accepted**
Bocelli, A. Because We Believe. The Best of Andrea Bocelli Vivere. Sugar Sr ©2007.CDSugar

5 **Chapter Ten, Young Prayer Warrior**
Passion of Christ. Dir. Mel Gibson. New Market Films, 2004, DVD 2007

6 **Chapter Fourteen, The Gift**
August Rush. Dir. Kirsten Sheridan. Warner Bros. Distribution, 2007, DVD 2008

7 **Chapter Nineteen, Senior Prom**
"I Hope You Dance", produced by Mark Wright and Randy Scruggs, written by Mark D. Sanders and Tia Sillers, MCA Publishing, A Division of Universal Studios, Inc. 2000